THE
ROMAN
EMPIRE IN
100
HAIKUS

THE ROMAN EMPIRE IN 100 HAIKUS

STUART LAYCOCK

WITH ILLUSTRATIONS BY
JOHN TRAVIS

AMBERLEY

First published 2019

Amberley Publishing
The Hill, Stroud
Gloucestershire, GL5 4EP

www.amberley-books.com

British Library Cataloguing in Publication Data.
A catalogue record for this book is available from the British Library.

ISBN 978 1 4456 9330 9 (paperback)
ISBN 978 1 4456 9331 6 (ebook)

Typeset in 10.5pt on 13pt Sabon.
Typesetting by Aura Technology and Software Services, India.
Printed in the UK.

Contents

Foreword by Dr Miles Russell

Of all periods in world history, the Roman Empire is probably one of the most endlessly fascinating, with its tales of aspiration, ambition, conquest and submission, standing shoulder to shoulder with the solid and enduring architecture of villas, towns, forts and erstwhile arenas of death which still dominate the land and townscapes of Western Europe, North Africa and East Asia. Rome is also, arguably, the most intensively studied of all ancient empires, so much so that one could legitimately ask whether there was anything new to say or whether there was any new perspective with which to help us understand, explain or illuminate this distinctive and rather peculiar society. The answer, of course, is a resounding 'yes', as is ably demonstrated in this engaging new work.

Stuart Laycock has set himself the considerable task of condensing the life of the Roman Empire through the medium of haiku. Outlining 100 key moments of ancient Roman history in a series of short observations using the English variant form of traditional Japanese poetry may, on the face of it, appear a somewhat curious project but, as Stuart demonstrates, deploying a restricted number of syllables helps to cut out all unnecessary and superfluous detail in order to identify what is really important. This is an intriguing and utterly beguiling approach to explaining the Empire of Rome both to a new audience and also to those who feel they are very familiar with the world of Augustus, Nero and Hadrian (other emperors are available). Sometimes humorous, sometimes melancholy, but always thought-provoking, these original poems take us on a journey across the centuries, proving that education and entertainment are not mutually exclusive. If only all history could be this much fun.

Dr Miles Russell
Senior Lecturer in Prehistoric and Roman Archaeology
Bournemouth University

Introduction

Human history, like human life itself, is complex and messy. It helps us get at least a grasp on some of it when it comes packaged in empire-sized chunks. The Persian Empire, the Chinese Empire, the Empire of Alexander the Great, the Aztec Empire, the Zulu Empire and, of course, the British Empire. All these will produce in most people an instant image of power, of military might, of conquest, of culture, of the mingling of different peoples and, often, of slaughter and cruelty. And in addition to all the empires which people have heard of, there are a host of other fascinating and formidable empires that deserve to be better known, like the great African empires of Ghana, Songhai, Oyo and Benin.

Still, if you had to choose one empire to sum up what empires can be, many, perhaps most, would choose the Roman Empire. It is a subject that cuts a great swathe across centuries of history and across thousands of miles. Its rise and fall is a great story-telling arc, one of humanity's most compelling, which encompasses within itself a myriad of smaller but equally compelling narratives.

Pretty much since its end, people have been asking, and still do 'What happened?' and 'What on earth did that mean?'

For much of history, the Roman Empire has been something for the ambitious and ruthless to emulate. Our words 'empire' and 'emperor' came, of course, from the Latin, and along with them came a whole iconography of power – of eagles, of purple, of marble statues and marble columns. Napoleon had his laurel wreath and his troops had their eagles. Notoriously, of course, in the 20th century, Italian dictator (another Latin word) Benito Mussolini, sought to build a new Roman Empire, commandeering that symbol of Roman power, the Fasces, thus giving us the word Fascism. Even Communist dictators were not immune to the iconography of Rome. Look at Ceausescu's colossal Palace of the Parliament in Bucharest. It has more than a touch of Stalinist taste about it, but ultimately it relies for its impact on the architecture of Imperial Rome.

Since the latter half of the twentieth century, of course, as the age of empires came to an end (at least for now) people have come to have a more nuanced view of Roman might. People's heroes have become perhaps more those rebels who fought Roman power, rather than those who imposed it; TV and movie figures like Ben Hur, Spartacus or Maximus Decimus Meridius in the film *Gladiator*. We should not, however, kid ourselves too much. We still live in an age where war is common, and competition in commercial spheres, even if it destroys livelihoods rather than actual lives, can be brutal and merciless. There is still a fascination with the naked exercise of power, and in an age of globalisation and global competition, there is still a fascination with how one entity managed to spread its control across a large chunk of the globe and, in some sense, unite a wide variety of different cultures and peoples for centuries before it finally vanished into the pages of history.

Some of the differences in how people across the globe regard the Roman Empire today are due to their ancestors' very different experiences of it, and the different role memories of it have played in the subsequent history of the region. If you are an Italian, for instance, you are probably going to have a rather different attitude to the Roman Empire than if you are, for instance, an Egyptian. And the British have their own particular take on this historical colossus, moulded both by Britain's experience within the Empire, but also by Britain's subsequent experience of running an even larger empire itself.

Britain was not a part of the core of the Roman Empire. On the contrary it was a small territory that was on the very margins of the Empire. It was conquered late in the process of imperial expansion by an emperor probably more interested in being able to claim a conquest than in any plans of what actually to do with Britain once Rome controlled it. Generally, Romans seem to have had comparatively little interest in, and enthusiasm for, what they regarded as this strange, remote island located somewhere out in the Atlantic. And many of the inhabitants of this island seem to have regarded the new power in their land with an equal lack of enthusiasm. One of our national heroines, is, of course, Boudicca, still to be seen driving her bronze chariot along the embankment by the Houses of Parliament. In her chariot, with her, are her daughters, whose rape by Romans was one of the motivations for Boudicca's rebellion.

Boudicca is still famous for slaughtering Romans, rather than for embracing the new culture Rome brought to these shores, and she was not alone in her distaste for what Rome had to offer. We tend to call the period Roman Britain, but in reality, the population of about half the land mass controlled by Rome in Britain did little to adopt Roman culture, preferring instead to continue their lives mostly as their ancestors had, long before Roman soldiers ever set foot on their shores. And that is even before we get to the vast swathes of what is now Scotland, which Rome never managed to control, a land where, if Rome ventured at all, it was but briefly before a retreat south to more easily defended territory.

The end of Roman Britain is traditionally seen as the Romans abandoning Britain, legionaries tramping onto ships in 410, perhaps waving a sad goodbye to an abandoned British wife or sweetheart and sailing off never to see Britain, or be seen by the British, again. In reality, as we shall see, the end of Roman control in Britain was a much messier and less formal affair - no hauling down and folding of a Roman standard as trumpet players blew. Indeed, it seems very likely that rather than Rome abandoning Britain, in fact, the ever rebellious Britain finally abandoned Rome. In either scenario, it was a divorce of sorts, a split that can be dated, not the same as the gradual fragmentation and collapse of Roman power that often marked the end of the empire elsewhere.

In the period after the end of Roman power in Britain, a new attitude to Rome would start to emerge. As new Anglo-Saxon kingdoms began to dominate what is now England, some of the Celtic Britons seeing British power restricted to parts of the west and north began to wonder whether rebelling against Rome had been such a good idea after all. Meanwhile, the new rulers of the Anglo-Saxon kingdoms began to adopt some of the imperial swagger of Rome to boost their power profile and own sense of self-importance.

The spread of Christianity across the land also gave a new perspective on the Roman Empire. Ther Empire was a persecutor of early martyrs, but also, ultimately, the Christian Roman Empire of Constantine the Great and subsequent emperors was seen as the foundation of the Roman Catholic spiritual and political empire that played such a huge role in medieval Europe.

Britain shared to some extent with the rest of Europe – a little later than some areas – the Renaissance fascination with exploring the secular side of Roman culture. However, what was to do most to shape attitudes to the Roman Empire in these islands was the growth of Britain's own empire.

Empires tend to share at least some similar problems. Above all, the imperial state must control vast numbers of people and impose foreign rule on them to its own benefit without permanent warfare, which would prove prohibitively costly in both blood and treasure. Humans being what they are, it also helps if the imperial power has a guiding sense of mission and destiny. This helps to unite domestic society at home and, to some extent, the ruled members of the empire too.

As Britain began seriously to expand its empire, in the 18th and 19th centuries, it moved beyond the early days of smash and grab foreign adventures into a more complex phase of attempting to build and sustain a large empire over huge distances. Its imperial elite read Greek and Latin classics at school and at university, and many of them would see parallels between the Roman experience of empire and their own.

They understood the need to get local elites on their side in order to make the task of controlling the empire feasible for an island off mainland Europe. They also increasingly understood the value both at home and abroad of the idea of the British Empire having a 'civilising' mission. Both the Roman and British empires were fundamentally built to conquer and exploit; but this harsh reality could be disguised by emphasising the 'benefits' that the imperial power could bring.

Rome could not, and did not, claim to bring civilisation to Greece, from where much of its own culture was drawn. However, it did see itself as bringing peace, stability, the rule of law, roads, and advanced urban and civil engineering to many areas absorbed into the empire. The British imperial elite saw themselves as playing a rather similar role, with an added dash of those core theoretical (if often slightly elusive, in practical terms) British values of 'fair play' and 'decency'.

Even when the empires were at their most powerful, though, such a sense of imperial mission was not strong enough to silence all critics of empire, either in Rome or Britain. As the British and other European empires neared their end, the voices deriding imperialism as a 'civilising' mission only grew and eventually silenced almost all expression of the concept. The shadow of that formerly dominant idea, that Britain spread civilisation across its empire, does, however, persist, and some of its assumptions still affect how many Britons look at their history. It also affects how many Britons look at the history of the Roman Empire.

Whatever your individual view of the Roman Empire, though, it is hard to deny that it still matters, in very real terms, today. Look at the Mediterranean basin and Europe, and because of that region's global influence, look around the world, and the legacy of Rome is everywhere.

Whether they are speaking Portuguese in Brazil, or French in Senegal, it is there in the Latin-derived languages in which they express themselves. Whether it is the Capitol Building in Washington or the Winter Palace in St. Petersburg, it is there in so many of the buildings that surround us, in aesthetics, as well as some construction techniques. It is there in art.

So much of European art derives directly or indirectly from the classical tradition. It is there in law, philosophy and literature. In each, Roman developments proved crucial in inspiring later European and global practitioners. It is there in military life. Rome's professional army and its campaigns were the antecedents of much of what we take for granted in a modern army. It is there in the names we give many of our children, like Clare, Anthony, Julia. And it is there in the human geography of Europe. So many of Europe's major towns and cities first became major towns and cities during the period of the Roman Empire.

The Empire at its greatest extent, of course, was not the product of some careful, long-term plan devised when Rome was tiny and then played out over many centuries. On the contrary, it was the result of numerous separate decisions, actions and accidents, where a single event, if it had taken a different course, might have sent the whole of Roman history in a very different direction.

Nobody now is entirely sure how and when Rome came into being. Most people have heard of the story of Romulus and Remus and Romans would later define 753 BC as the year in which Rome was founded. Early Rome was ruled by kings, but according to Roman tradition, in 509 BC, the last king of Rome, Lucius Tarquinius Superbus, was toppled, and Rome became a republic, with two annually elected consuls taking power.

The Mediterranean world into which the young Roman Republic was born was a crowded one, with numerous different cultures and entities competing for commercial, military and political advantage. In Italy itself, the young Rome had a large number of competitors, including the Etruscans and Samnites. To the east, the city states of Greece, places like Athens, Sparta, Thebes and Corinth, were about to reach their greatest period of political, cultural and military development. Further to the east Cyrus the Great had not long previously conquered the Median, Lydian and Babylonian empires to establish the mighty Persian Empire. At around the time Rome became a Republic, Persia would seize control of the mighty Egyptian Empire. Phoenician influence had spread the length of the Mediterranean and the Phoenicians had already founded a colony in Africa that the Roman Republic would come to know well, Carthage. In the north of Italy and beyond the Alps lay fierce tribes of Gauls and other Celts. And this is not even the full list of competitors the young Roman Republic had in the Mediterranean basin.

The story of how the Roman Republic went from being a tiny Italian entity to one of the ancient world's major powers is, of course, hugely complex, but it is worth mentioning a few key points at this stage, to set the scene for our journey through the history of the Empire later.

In the late 5th century BC, Rome started on the path to building a vast empire by fighting local wars. The venture was in danger almost before it had begun. In the early 4th century BC, Gauls moving south from northern Italy, sacked Rome. The Romans, however, picked themselves and once again started trying to expand their area of control in Latium and Etruria. The Latin War of 340-338 BC resulted in the end of the Latin League and the Romans taking control of its territory. It was small-scale compared to what was about to happen to the east. In 334 BC Alexander of Macedon invaded the Persian Empire at the start of a venture that would see him build an empire that stretched from Greece to Afghanistan and the borders of India. After Alexander's premature death, however, Alexander's empire would rapidly fragment, while to the west Rome's realms would, with occasional temporary reverses, keep on growing.

Three wars in Italy against the Samnites followed. The Samnites were a powerful confederation and victory against them did not come easy for Rome. There would also be war with Pyrrhus of Epirus, from across the Adriatic, and his allies among the Greek cities of southern Italy. Costly 'victories' for Pyrrhus gave us the phrase 'Pyrrhic victory' and in the end, Rome found itself the dominant power in the Italian peninsula. It was not, however, the only power in that region of the Mediterranean. To the south, the mighty, commercially rich city state of Carthage, with its powerful fleets, also had a thirst for land. The island of Sicily, strategically located both to Rome's Italian possessions and the core of the Carthaginian Empire, would turn rivalry between Rome and Carthage into outright warfare.

The long, bitter First Punic War from 264 to 241 BC, saw Rome eventually defeat Carthage and seize Sicily. It was, however, just the beginning of a long life and death battle between the two great Mediterranean powers. The Second Punic War fought from 218 to 201 BC saw Hannibal invade Italy, smash three Roman armies in three major victories and reach the gates of Rome, before the tide of war turned and Carthage was once again defeated. Rome seized territory previously held by Carthage in Spain. From 149 to 146 BC, Rome would finally smash Carthaginian power in the Third Punic War. It would capture and destroy the city itself and occupy more land in north Africa.

Rome was send troops eastwards as well, fighting the Illyrian wars and wars against Macedonia and other powers. In the same year they burned Carthage, they also burned Corinth in Greece.

Roman power reached across into the Middle East as well. In 190 BC at the Battle of Magnesia a Roman army smashed the army of Antiochus III, ruler of the Seleucid Empire, one of the successor states to the Empire of Alexander the Great. Mithridates the Great of Pontus would give the Roman Republic some scary moments in the wars he fought against it in the first half of the 1st century BC, but in the end he, too, could not stand against the might of Rome.

And Rome was also on the move in Europe, expanding out of the Italian peninsula to west, north and east. Its forces advanced into southern Gaul. It was advancing in Spain too.

However, for all its military successes abroad, Rome could still have major problems much closer to home. The Social Wars were nothing like as friendly as they sound. The term 'Social' here is derived from the Latin word 'socii' or 'allies'. Rome's Italian allies, discontented with their lot within the Roman world, rebelled. Rome was eventually militarily triumphant but was forced to make major concessions.

Rome faced a number of major slave rebellions in Sicily and Italy in the 2nd and 1st centuries BC. The most famous of these was, of course, the third war, which started in 73 BC when the ex-gladiator Spartacus became prominent as one of the rebel leaders. The Romans suffered some significant problems in coping with the rebellion but in the end, it, too, was crushed.

Increasingly though, Rome's problems in the late Republic came not from outside the system but from within. Rome's very successes against its enemies helped thrust into the limelight a series of ambitious, ruthless generals, with the power, money, fame and contacts to change their aims from serving the Republic to running it. And when two or more such generals found themselves competing for power and authority the results could be particularly catastrophic.

In the early 1st century BC Marius and Sulla, both successful commanders against Rome's enemies, would fight it out for pre-eminence in the Republic itself. And they would be followed by Pompey and Caesar. Pompey had major military successes against Rome's enemies in the East. Caesar ruthlessly and brutally expanded Roman control in Gaul. In the end they would battle for control of Rome and Caesar would win. His assassination, however, would usher in a new generation of warlords battling for control of Rome, and out of those wars, would, in the end, come the Empire.

I have long loved the history of the Roman Empire. It is a big, succulent slice of the story of humanity, and within it there is something to suit almost everybody's tastes and interests.

When I was a young and studying Latin I was fortunate enough to be helped by my parents to collect Roman coins. The coin catalogue I acquired had brief biographies of all the emperors, empresses, imperial children and usurpers who appear on Roman coins. For a then rather sheltered youth it was a fascinating introduction to a world of violence and profligacy of all types on a huge scale. In my adulthood I have been fortunate to write on assorted aspects of the history of the Roman Empire, and take a more rounded look at the complexities of this fascinating period.

I have also been fortunate enough to enjoy writing and reading poetry. The haiku is originally a Japanese form, but is now widely in use around the word. It is fascinating to adopt in a historical context because its use of so few syllables forces the writer to try to decide exactly what is most important to say about the subject. What will you spend your few syllables on saying? It's a fresh and unusual approach to the Empire, but it seemed to me that the haiku form is ideal for examining this age, for probing it. Some people are put off reading poems because they feel poetry is not for them, but sometimes poetry can just be about saying what needs to be said, how it needs to be said.

Choosing just 100 subjects to try to sum up the vast pageant of tragedy, comedy, excitement, brutality, culture, sensitivity, callousness, peace, war, victory and defeat that was the Roman Empire was never going to be easy, but again it has forced me to think hard about what I see as some of the more interesting and meaningful stories from that amazing period. Much, inevitably, has had to be left out, but I hope you will find some of what I have included fresh to you and interesting. It was quite a journey for the Romans. I hope you will enjoy this brief poetic dip into it.

The entries are arranged very roughly in a chronological order where that's practical, but I have inserted into the framework entries which cover a wide time period where it seemed best. So if you read from beginning to end you will get a broad sense of how the Empire progressed. Or just dip into any subject that takes your fancy, if you prefer.

Thanks to Connor Stait at Amberley for believing in this somewhat unusual approach to Roman history and helping the project through to completion and thanks to John Travis for his brilliant drawings, which bring the subject to life visually as powerfully as I hope the text does poetically and historically.

The End of the Republic

For the end, Janus,
is a beginning, and dark
lies beyond the door.

The Romans were very well aware of their history, and had a strong sense of their own achievements. By the mid-1st century BC Rome had risen from mud hut village to being by far the most powerful state in Europe and the Mediterranean basin. During that journey the Republic had encountered numerous difficulties, but, in the end, by pluck, by luck, by trick, or by sheer endurance and determination had conquered a host of enemies from one end of Europe to the other and beyond. Roman historians listed the triumphs in their books. Yet Rome in the mid-1st century BC was also a society in deep crisis. Admiration for Rome's victorious generals was at the core of the Roman tradition; the generals had kept Rome safe and had conquered its enemies. However, in the 1st century they would tear it apart. First Marius and Sulla would battle for dominance, then Caesar and Pompey, then it would be Octavian and Mark Antony against the killers of Caesar. Then Octavian against Mark Antony. And that is just listing the main civil wars, not the other more minor ones. The process could not go on. Some kind of solution was going to have to be found.

Actium, 31 BC

Octavian proud
Antony and lover prowed,
dreams of power rammed.

If you had to ask people to name one Roman battle, then Actium would be the one named by many. It has so much. It has the story of Cleopatra, a battle for control of the Roman world, and, of course, dramatic sea combat that looks impressive on the movie screen. In reality, this brutal battle in which so many died horribly was a key event in Roman history. Having defeated their rivals for power in the Roman world, on 2 September 31 BC Octavian fought Mark Antony and his partner (in both senses) Cleopatra. Actium or Aktion was on the north-west coast of Greece, a little south of Corfu. There is now an Aktion Airport there. Antony and Cleopatra were there with their combined fleet in a position threatening Italy, just a short distance away across the Adriatic. Octavian's forces in Greece began to threaten Antony's position and eventually the two fleets met for the decisive battle. The fleets attempted to outflank each other and there was some bitter fighting, but Cleopatra finally withdrew with her forces, and Antony managed to escape and follow her. Antony's land and sea forces in the area then surrendered. Antony subsequently killed himself and so did Cleopatra. In the end Octavian was master of the Roman world, and Egypt too.

Augustus becomes Emperor

From beneath the cloak
of the Republic the boot
of an Emperor.

The troubled Roman Republic did not become an Empire overnight. Rome was deeply imbued with Republican ideology. One of its key early legends was its rejection of the last King of Rome, Tarquin the Proud, and the establishment of a republic that by the time of Octavian had lasted almost 500 years. Rome had fought and conquered many foreign kings and come to view the very idea of kingship as self-evidently inferior to that of a republic. So the process by which Augustus assumed near complete power and turned Republic into Empire was a gradual one, in which extensive efforts were made to cloak his extension of power in republican constitutional terms and make it seem in some sense a logical development of the Republic. Officially power remained with the authorities of the Republic, like the Senate, but starting in 27 BC Octavian had himself granted key political and military powers for life. He changed his name to Augustus, the August one, to reflect his new status and rather than call himself king he took the title Princeps, principal citizen. He also used the title Imperator, 'Commander', traditionally in Roman history a title given to successful generals. It, along with the titles Caesar and Augustus, were retained by later emperors, 'emperor' being a word that itself derives from Imperator. Just as Octavian himself had acquired authority by being adopted by Julius Caesar, so Augustus himself first adopted his own grandsons Gaius and Lucius Caesar and after they died at an early age he adopted Tiberius, already his stepson.

A Roman Expedition to Yemen, 26 BC

The sands are thirsty
they suck dreams of imperial
power dry as skulls.

Not all military efforts by Augustus would be successful. Aelius Gallus was a prefect of Egypt in 26-24 BC. Augustus thought it would be a good idea to send him into the Arabian desert to extend Roman power and influence there and to get his hands on silver, gold, frankincense and myrrh. The expedition wasn't a great success; indeed it wasn't really a success at all. The Greek philosopher, geographer and historian Strabo, perhaps relying on what Gallus himself said, blames the local guide for the failure of the expedition, which may or may not be true. The basic problem seems to have been that Gallus ended up marching his troops for months across barren desert with little or no access to water. When he finally reached what is now Yemen, he only managed to besiege the target city there for six days before his troops ran out of water and had to retreat. He ended up eventually in Egypt again, having lost only seven men from enemy action, but many more from sickness, starvation and thirst.

Virgil's *Aeneid*

Arms and the man you
sing sugar legend to minds
hungry for empire.

Every empire, if it is really to prosper, needs a sense of destiny. It needs a sense of where it has come from and where it is going. Starting writing probably shortly after the Battle of Actium, the poet Virgil set out to give Rome exactly that. Romans had long been in awe of Greek culture, its myths, its legends, its literature. *The Iliad* and *Odyssey* were well-known by Romans and well-loved. Publius Vergilius Maro was a poet who had already written works inspired by Greek originals. He now set out to become Rome's Homer. Julius Caesar had made much of his supposed descent from Venus and her son Aeneas by the Trojan Anchises. Virgil set out in the *Aeneid*, a sort of combined Roman *Odyssey* and *Iliad*, to show Aeneas escaping across the sea after the sack of Troy and then landing in Italy and fighting to establish the foundations of the society that would become Rome. For a society that had come through long periods of civil war and now hoped Augustus would build a new, better Rome, the subtext was clear. And if it wasn't, Virgil helpfully wrote that on the shield of Aeneas were portrayed scenes from the history of the Julian clan, including Augustus and Agrippa conquering Cleopatra at Actium, alongside portraits of distant lands and rivers reached by Rome's armies, including the Rhine and the Euphrates. The *Aeneid* became one of the key texts of Roman imperialism.

Roman Religion

Wide smile of Empire
thinking its gods goddesses
bless Rome's bravery.

The core of Roman religion in the Early Empire was a combination of Italic and Greek religious beliefs and practices. Among the more specifically Italic elements were deities connected with the home, like Vesta, goddess of the hearth, and the Lares and Penates. The combined classical pantheon included a range of major deities with Roman names who were assimilated with their Greek counterparts. Thus Jupiter was Zeus, Juno was Hera, Venus was Aphrodite, Mars was Ares, etc. Across the Empire, local religions that had existed before the Romans arrived would continue and often some of those deities might be combined with Roman deities to produce hybrid gods and goddesses. Roman religion played a key role in Romans' perception of their state and its place in the world. The emperors were Pontifex Maximus, chief priest. Roma herself was worshipped as a goddess. Deification of rulers had started in Greek culture, with, for instance, Alexander the Great being worshipped after his death. Some of the Roman emperors would adopt this idea themselves, with unbridled enthusiasm.

Conquests by Augustus

The eagles take wing
they have seen tasty morsels
they swoop, no mercy.

It is one of the ironies of history that much of what we know as the Roman Empire actually came under Roman control during the Republic. Augustus, however, did quite a lot to extend the boundaries of Roman power during and after his assumption of imperial power. In Asia Minor, Galatia was gobbled up when king Amyntas was killed by the widow of someone he had killed. Client king Herod Achelaus was deposed, and Judaea was brought under direct Roman control. In North Africa, the borders of Roman control were expanded east, south and west. Augustus completed the Roman conquest of the Iberian peninsula in ten years of bitter fighting against the northern Cantabri and Astures tribes. He conquered the Alpine tribes and his armies advanced in Illyricum, Pannonia, Raetia and Germany. By the time of his death in AD 14, with the exception of a few client kingdoms along its borders like Thrace, which would be gobbled up later, and a few later additions like parts of Britain and Dacia, the Roman Empire was looking very much like the Roman Empire we are used to.

Rome's Slaves

Unwilling Atlas
you hold empire aloft with
pain blood fear sweat death.

By the beginning of the Empire, Rome had long been a society that relied heavily on slavery. Rome's wars of conquest in the late Republic had brought in hundreds of thousands of captives, many of whom ended up as slaves. With supply so abundant, slaves became cheaper and more widely used. They were everywhere, from farms and workplaces to places of entertainment, in the home and in the imperial household. Many slaves did basic manual labour but some slaves were highly educated and acted as, for instance, tutors and secretaries. During the Empire it is estimated that something like ten per cent of the population of the Empire's towns consisted of slaves. The sudden influx of slaves in the late Republic helped lead to the conditions that created slave rebellions such as the one led by Spartacus. By the time of the Empire, the slave economy had been longer established and rebellions were much less of a problem for Rome. For many slaves life was nasty, brutish and short. Some slaves, however, prospered in Roman society and slaves could become free by the process of manumission. Freedom could be granted by a master out of gratitude or respect, or could be bought, and some freedmen became prosperous, successful and established in Roman society. The poet Horace, for instance, was the son of a freedman.

Ovid and the Art of Love

Lovers' lines poet,
no emperor's love for you,
embrace your exile.

Roman literature is one of the foundations of modern western literature. Some of its love poetry still strikes home today. Take, for instance, the famous anguished poem 85 by Catullus, 'Odi et Amo'. 'I hate. I love. You might ask why I'd do that. I don't know. But I know that I do and it hurts so bad.' It feels as fresh today as when it was written (and sounds much better in the original elegiac couplets). The poet Ovid wrote some pretty racy poems as well. They include Amores 1.5 in which he describes a visit by his mistress Corinna which ends as you might expect, and his Ars Amatoria (the Art of Love) has suggestions on different sex positions. In the year 8 Augustus banished Ovid from Rome to what is now Constanta in Romania. Ovid had written some major works including the Metamorphoses, which have been hugely influential over the centuries. Augustus may not have been a fan (though Shakespeare was) but nevertheless, banishment was fairly extreme criticism and Ovid's suggestion that he was exiled for 'a poem and an error' has led to speculation that some of his racier poetry may have severely offended the more socially conservative inclinations of Augustus.

Slaughter in the Teutoburg Forest, AD 9

Amidst fierce forests
crow feast, bleached bones, rotting kit
dead dreams of empire.

Augustus had generally had a very successful military career, but a few years before his death, some of his forces suffered one of the worst military disasters in Roman history in a battle that may have changed the future of Europe. It was a disaster inflicted on the Romans by somebody they had themselves trained. It was a Roman custom to take as 'hostage' children of leaders of enemies they had, at least, partly subdued. The advantage was twofold. Roman possession of the children inhibited the enemies from further action against Rome. It also allowed them to bring up the children as little Romans so, when grown up, the children would, it was hoped, be pro-Roman. Arminius of the Chersuci in Germany was such a hostage. He did not turn out as Rome hoped. By the time he returned to Germany he knew what it would take to beat the Romans. He secretly formed an alliance of tribes and then lured Publius Quinctilus Varus with three legions and auxiliary troops into an ambush in the Teutoburg Forest. Varus and his army were annihilated and recent archaeological finds near Kalkreise suggest the viciousness of the fighting. The defeat may have inhibited further Roman expansion eastwards and allowed Germany to develop differently to Roman-controlled Europe. Certainly it became a powerful symbol for German nationalism in the 19th century. In the years after the slaughter, Augustus is said from time to time have groaned and muttered 'Varus, give me back my legions.'

Sejanus and Tiberius

An old goat lost in
capricious Capri capers
still his horns are sharp.

The quality of government offered by autocracy hugely depends, obviously, on the quality of the autocrat. After the chaos of the civil wars of the late Republic, it is probably fair to say that the rule of Augustus offered a few benefits to set against the many inherent problems of dictatorship. By contrast, the rule of Tiberius, second emperor of Rome, showed up many of the disadvantages. Tiberius had been an extremely successful military commander. He would not be a successful emperor. He seems to have become massively disillusioned with the role and chosen a life of semi-retirement in a pleasure palace on the island of Capri, leaving others to jostle for power in Rome. Chief among those jostling was Sejanus, commander of the Praetorian Guard. After the death of Drusus, son of Tiberius, Sejanus took centre stage, helped by his lover, Livilla, who had been married to Drusus. Sejanus secured his position by removing those who might be a threat to it. For a time Tiberius didn't seem to know or care, lost in his pleasures on Capri. Suetonius gives a lurid description of these, claiming they included an extensive collection of pornography and erotic art including a painting in his bedroom by Parrhasius of the virgin huntress Atalanta pleasuring the hero Meleager. Sejanus was aiming to be the heir of Tiberius or perhaps even replace him. Then Tiberius suddenly turned against him. A letter from Tiberius read out in the senate denounced Sejanus. Sejanus was executed in 31, and close friends and associates of Sejanus were also subsequently purged.

Annona, Free Grain for Rome

Rome greedy for grain
annona anaesthetize
keeping poor quiet.

Most successful empires make at least some limited attempt to spread wealth. Already under the Republic, Rome's rulers had realised that a hungry population in Rome was a dangerous population. Their solution was first to subsidise grain distribution to the poor and then to hand it out for free. Under the Empire it is estimated that something like 200,000 people in Rome were receiving such free grain or bread. This process that Romans called the *annona* was a huge logistical operation that involved large numbers of bulk grain carriers bringing supplies across the Mediterranean from Egypt and North Africa. On arrival at a major port like Portus the grain ships would be unloaded and the grain transported in smaller vessels up the Tiber to Rome. Roman crowds did still sometimes take an active part in imperial politics. However, the *annona* played a part in controlling one of the major potential causes of instability in Rome. The satirist Juvenal famously declared that people had given up their political rights and passions and were only interested in 'panem at circenses', bread and circuses.

The Death of Caligula, AD 41

Your little boots wade
deep in the dark crimson wave
soon brimful bloody.

It would be fair to say Caligula has not been noted in history as an example of good governance. Many of the accounts by ancient authors may have been affected by political hostility to him. Some of what it is said may be exaggerated. However, it still seems hard to see Caligula as anything other than an example of what happens when total power gets into the wrong hands. Caligula (real name Gaius, Caligula, 'little boots,' was a nickname he was given from dressing up as a soldier when a child) came to power in 37 after the death of his great-uncle, Tiberius. He seems to have been keen on portraying himself as a god. He is accused of incest, particularly with his sister Drusilla. He is said to have pretty much taken any woman he wanted, including a bride about to be married. He would invite couples to dinner then select wives for his private attention in another room before returning them to their husbands with comments on their performance. He is said to have been capriciously murderous, ordering the death of anyone he suspected of disloyalty, or often just for fun. According to Suetonius, when kissing his wife or girlfriend he would say, 'Off comes this pretty head when I command.' If even a quarter of it is true he was definitely not a nice person. And he spent recklessly on luxuries and extravagance. In the end, in 41, after less than four years in power, he was stabbed to death by conspirators – the first of so many Roman emperors to end like that.

Messalina

Lust and not lost to
history, queen of passion,
who were you really?

People do like to gossip. They particularly like to gossip about people
more famous than themselves, and the Romans were no exception. Over
the centuries Roman empresses came in for a lot of gossip, with plenty
of accusations of inappropriate behaviour. Accusations of affairs were
commonplace. It's hard now to know how seriously to take many of these
accusations. Fake news is not a new invention and some of the rumours
could have been politically motivated. On the other hand, in a society
where marriage was often not for love, where the imperial household
represented absolute power and where the emperor was himself often
engaged in satisfying his lust elsewhere, it is far from impossible that
some empresses were also enjoying themselves in this respect. Messalina,
third wife of the emperor Claudius, comes in for particular attention
from Roman historians in this respect. She is accused of having numerous
lovers and in one particularly scandalous story which has caused
considerable comment over the centuries she is accused in the *Natural
History* of Pliny the Elder of competing against a famous prostitute to
see who could have sex the most times continuously. Messalina allegedly
won with a score of 25. Having actually married one of her lovers, she
was killed in 48.

Nero and Music

You pluck the strings of
history too tunelessly
discord in empire.

Nero, successor to Claudius, had many unappealing sides, but he did at least love music. Music is so evocative that a single piece can often evoke the feeling of an entire age, whether it is medieval plainsong, an Elizabethan madrigal, a piece of Georgian music, or something from the 20th century, 1950s rock or 1990s pop. By comparison we sadly know much less about the tunes which Romans played and listened to. A variety of educated guesses can be made about how Roman music sounded and plainsong is thought to have origins in the late Roman period, but we don't have ready access to a catalogue of Roman tunes. We do, however, know that music was important to them, both from literary references and from depictions of Roman musicians. And we know that some of the emperors were keen on displaying their musical talents (or otherwise), particularly Nero. Nero sang on stage, played the cithara and took an interest in musical technology like the water organ. He is, of course, said to have 'fiddled while Rome burned', or at least to have sung 'The Sack of Ilium' in costume while it burned. Nero was, in many respects, a terrible emperor. This, however, may well be anti-Nero fake news. The historian Tacitus says that Nero rushed from Antium where he was at the time of the fire to help with relief efforts, brought in grain and opened his gardens and public buildings to those made homeless. Stories, though, that he had sung during the fire were already abroad among the population.

Agrippina and Poppaea

You play the fatal
game of imperial hurdles
until face meets floor.

Under Nero, two formidable women would each aim for control of the emperor. One of the women involved had already been fighting imperial battles for a long time. Agrippina the Younger was a captive of imperial politics from the start. She had powerful imperial connections through both parents. Then in March 37, her brother Gaius would become Rome's third emperor and later the same year she would have a son, the future emperor Nero. She found herself involved in the chaos and carnage of Caligula's regime. Rumours accused her, along with her sisters, of committing incest with him. After his death and the death of Messalina, wife of the emperor Claudius, she married him, despite being his niece. She now ensured that Claudius adopted her son as his heir. When Claudius died, some said she had poisoned him. She did make sure that her son, Nero, inherited power. With her son on the throne, Agrippina might have felt she had secured a safe position of power and wealth. She was wrong. Her son started looking to other favourites, male and female. Agrippina tried to control him, maybe even plot against him. At some stage a woman called Poppaea Sabina became Nero's fascination and mistress. Nero plotted to kill his mother with a collapsing, sinkable boat and when that failed, he had her killed in a more conventional fashion. His wife Octavia was killed, Poppaea got a divorce and married Nero. However, Poppaea's ex-husband, Otho, would later play a part in the fall of Nero. He would get his revenge.

Boudicca's Rebellion, AD 60-61

Woman demanding
a red vengeance for her own,
eagles' rule is rocked.

Julius Caesar first took a Roman army to Britain decades before the Empire. He found an elusive enemy and terrible weather and his efforts achieved little. Claudius, third Emperor of Rome, had more success. His troops landed, smashed the British forces that stood against them and established Roman control of a corner of Britain. From here, with the support of client British kings, they would start to expand their territory. The strategic logic would be, as with somewhere like the Iberian peninsula, to occupy all of Britain and then move most forces elsewhere to new conquests. But Britain would never be entirely conquered by Rome, and in 60 or 61 a British queen would give Nero and his empire a sign of what was to come. The widow of Prasutagus, King of the Iceni, had experienced the worst of Rome. Loan sharks had taken much of the tribe's money, land had been confiscated, her daughters had been raped. Her tribe and some allies rose in rebellion, burning a string of the cities built in Britain since the Roman invasion. She inflicted a humiliating defeat on Roman forces sent against her. The Roman presence in Britain looked in danger until Suetonius Paulinus managed to get Boudicca to fight him on ground favourable to his troops. In the end, Roman discipline and strategic experience won out over British bravery and ferocity, but it had been close.

Roman Expeditions into Africa

Two worlds reaching out
stomping sands and daring dunes
fingers touch, arms clash.

The Roman Empire was very largely a Mediterranean Empire. The Mediterranean, offering sea routes that were often quicker and more convenient than land travel, united its main territories. The Empire struggled to advance militarily and politically too far from *Mare Nostrum* (our sea). In the north it failed to penetrate far into Germany. In the east, it never managed to replace Parthian and Persian power and build an empire deep inside Asia. In Africa, it never managed to expand across the Sahara. But that doesn't mean it didn't probe the region. A number of Roman military expeditions reached into Africa far to the south of the northern coastal strip. In 20 BC, Cornelius Balbus led an expedition deep into the Libyan desert against the Garamantes, and celebrated a triumph on his return. In 42, Suetonius Paulinus attacked desert raiders in what is now south-eastern Morocco. Other expeditions against the Garamantes followed. It is hard to know whether any elements of these expeditions managed to cross the Sahara, but trans-Sahara trade routes did exist, and in 90, a Roman called Julius Maternus, perhaps a merchant or diplomat, travelled from the Libyan coast to the land of Agisymba, where he encountered rhinoceroses. A mosaic at Villa Romana del Casale at Piazza Armerina in Sicily shows a captured rhinoceros being handled by Roman soldiers in the early 4th century. In the east, in 66 Nero sent centurions far south to explore the Upper Nile.

Celebrity Gladiators

Alive, dead, behead
on bloodthirsty sand slaughtered
crowd crows scream for more.

Few of us can think of many worse jobs than being forced to fight regular duels, at the risk of our own lives, purely for the entertainment of a crowd. It is true that for many gladiators life was unpleasant, terrifying, painful and short. The best-known gladiator today is Spartacus, who along with a group of others decided that a gladiatorial life was definitely not for them and escaped and rebelled. However, a bit like football stars of today, some gladiators became hugely rich and popular with Roman crowds because of their success in the arena. The future emperor Tiberius, for instance, is said to have paid some famous retired gladiators 100,000 sesterces each to appear in his games. Nero is said to have given the gladiator Spiculus land and buildings equal to those of generals who had celebrated triumphs. Martial wrote a poem about the gladiators Priscus and Verus who fought in the Colosseum's inaugural games. And just as some women today want to be football WAGs, many women then wanted a gladiator. The poet Juvenal refers to a senator's wife Eppia running off to Egypt with her gladiator lover, Sergius. Most celebrity gladiators were men, but Juvenal does also mention one well-known woman gladiator called Mevia who, one breast bare like the mythical Amazons, fought boars in the arena. Nero allegedly took it all a bit further as he so often did. Allegedly he would dress as a wild beast, 'attack' the genitals of men and women tied to stakes and then be attended to by his lover Doryphorus.

Hero of Alexandria

Engineer hero,
manufacture future brain
genius machine.

The Roman world was really quite advanced in terms of science. Hero is a great name. He can also be referred to as Heron of Alexandria but that is not quite as much fun, and in many scientific senses he was a hero. Hero was heroic in the mid-1st century in Alexandria. The city was one of the intellectual power houses of the ancient world and Hero could draw on the mathematical and engineering work of Babylonia, Egypt and the Greek world to inspire him and help him in his work. Hero wrote widely on mathematics, mechanics, pneumatics and physics, but he is perhaps best known today for his writings on innovative mechanical devices. His work, the *Pneumatica*, describes such inventions as singing birds, a coin-operated machine, and an organ powered by a windmill. He is, however, best known for a device that represents one of the great 'what ifs' of history. Hero's 'Aeolopile' is effectively the first steam engine in history. A sphere mounted on a shaft and with two nozzles pointing in opposite directions sat over a fire filled with a water. As the water boiled and produced steam, the steam flowing out of the two nozzles turned the sphere on its axle. How would the Roman Empire and the world have been different if Hero had realised the full potential of the steam engine 1700 years before the industrial revolution?

The Year of the Four Emperors, AD 69

Four men hold the year
grabbed hard by their grip-clenched hand
death for all but one.

In 68, Nero's eccentric rule was finally terminated. Abandoned by the Senate and the Praetorian Guard, he was toppled from power, and with the dynasty founded by Augustus now finished, a bitter power struggle began in the Year of the Four Emperors. First on the imperial throne after Nero was Galba, whose power base had been Spain. Accompanying and supporting him was Otho, Governor of Lusitania, who had previously lost his wife Poppaea to Nero. Galba then managed to upset the German legions, who promptly chose Vitellius as their emperor. Galba attempted to firm up senate support by choosing an heir to their liking, thus also upsetting Otho, who had other ideas. On 15 January 69, the Praetorians killed Galba and made Otho emperor, in Rome at least. With Vitellius advancing south, Otho headed north to fight him. In the first Battle of Bedriacum near Cremona in northern Italy in April 69 Otho lost to Vitellius and killed himself. Vitellius now took power in Rome, but the changes of 69 were not finished yet. Vitellius failed to win the support of various sections of the army, and troops in the Balkans made Vespasian their emperor. In October at the Second Battle of Bedriacum the forces of Vitellius were this time defeated. Vitellius was killed in December as Vespasian's troops entered Rome to start the Flavian dynasty that would provide Rome's next three emperors and some stability.

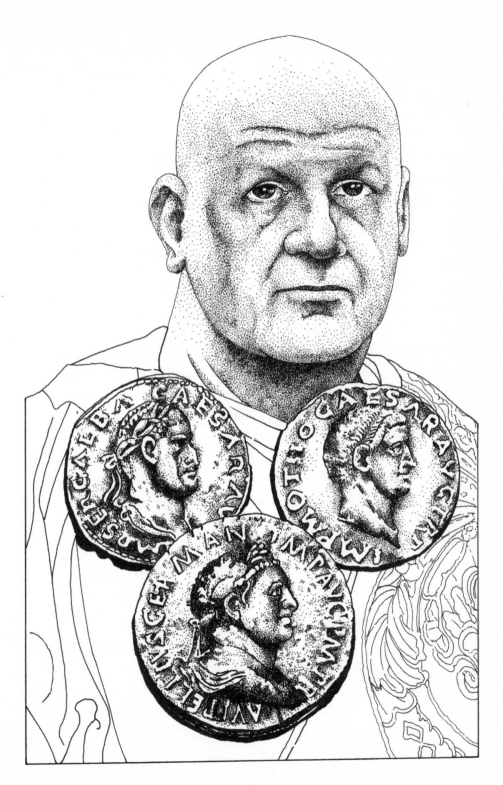

Chariot Racing Teams

Clamour of keen hooves
mouths roaring the passion in
fan's hearts shouts thunder.

If you think passion for team sports and sports hooliganism is a modern phenomenon, you'd be wrong. Chariot racing had, of course, long existed in Greece, including in the ancient Olympic games, but it reached new levels in Rome. The racing chariots were divided into four factions, or teams, distinguished by colours as football teams are today. The four classic Roman teams were the Reds, Whites, Blues and Greens. Just as football supporters are fanatical about their teams, so were ancient Roman chariot racing fans. At one point the poet Juvenal writes that a loss by the Greens could plunge Rome into despair. Like football stars today, successful Roman chariot racing stars also could become hugely famous and popular, could switch between teams, and could make vast fortunes. Gaius Appuleius Diocles, for instance, in a career that saw him drive for three different teams, won almost 36 million sesterces, a colossal figure. Chariot racing, however, was rather more dangerous than football so many drivers died young. And chariot-racing fan violence could be on a massive scale. Among the most famous incidents were the Nika riots in Constantinople in 532. The emperor's attempts to punish fans of the blue and green teams for fighting each other, along with discontent with the government generally, united the factions in violent rioting that ended with thousands of deaths and quite a lot of the city destroyed.

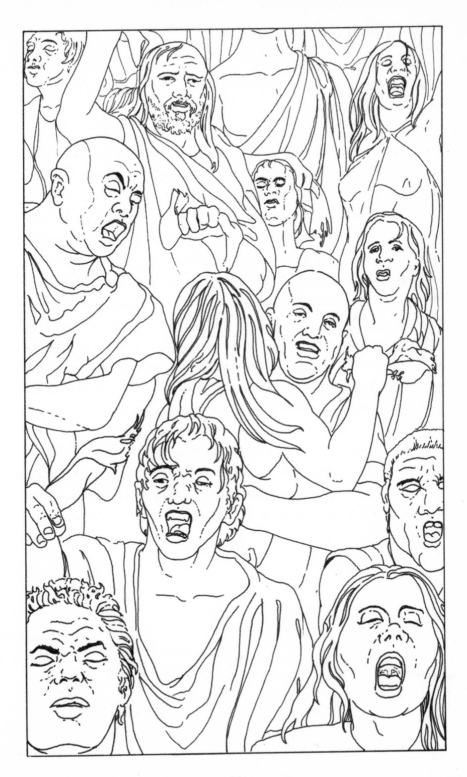

Hair Fashions for Women

Crowned women's crowning
glory, an empire of tastes,
the waves rule Roma.

Today most women put some effort into keeping their hair looking as they want it, occasionally measuring their own look against what is fashionable and making adjustments as they see fit. Roman women's fashion in clothing changed generally far more slowly than modern fashions. Roman women, however, did love to do their hair, and what rich Roman women may have lacked in terms of modern conveniences like hair dryers and straighteners they more than made up for with the added input their hair received from slaves and servants. Fashions changed over the centuries and, no doubt, as now, women noticed what the rich and famous did with their hair. In the Augustan period imperial woman might have gone for a simple, 'classical' look. As the 1st century wore on more elaborate looks appeared, like the tight curls of Poppaea, or the amazing tiara of curls that crowned (almost literally) the head of Domitia. In the late second century and the third century a sort of sculpted Marcel wave very similar to fashions from the 1920s and 1930s was very popular with imperial women. In the late 3rd century this was replaced by something more controlled and hard-edged, and in the 4th and 5th century, as the Roman imperial family became Christian, the look was rather neat and businesslike, probably trying to reflect a more 'modest' look.

The Fall of Jerusalem, AD 70

Golden city shines
your glow is smeared with crimson
now smoke hides your face.

There were many reasons the Jewish people were never going to be easy for Rome to rule, but the huge difference in the Jewish and the Roman attitudes to religion was a prime one. The area had seen a number of violent incidents in the 1st century, but then in 66 disputes over taxation and religion between Jews and the Roman authorities led to a full-scale Jewish rebellion. The Romans were thrown out of Jerusalem and a major Roman expeditionary force under Cestius Gallus suffered a massive defeat at the Battle of Beth Horon, with thousands of Romans dead. The Jewish revolutionary government became the dominant force in the region. In response, Nero sent the (then) future emperor Vespasian to re-establish Roman control. In a ruthless campaign, Vespasian took control of Galilee and then pushed on to other targets. When Vespasian's imperial ambitions eventually took him elsewhere, his son Titus took control in 70 of besieging Jerusalem. The siege was a long and bitter one, in which both the male and female inhabitants of Jerusalem fought to keep the Romans out of their city. In the end, weakened by hunger, the defenders, despite savage fighting, were unable to prevent the Romans breaking into and taking the city. Jerusalem was burned, people were killed, enslaved, scattered, the Temple was looted and destroyed. The Arch of Titus in Rome shows the Temple treasures being carried in triumph by the Romans.

The Colosseum

Die-nasty advert
for colossal dynasty
fame v infamy.

History plays some funny tricks. One of the most instantly recognisable sites of Rome and indeed of the world is the Colosseum, that vast amphitheatre, the ruins of which dominate a chunk of the modern city and which are represented in tourist souvenirs now residing in homes the world over. As with many great buildings, the Colosseum was designed to glorify the rich and powerful men who organised and paid for its construction. Its official name was the Flavian Amphitheatre, to commemorate the three emperors of the Flavian dynasty, Vespasian and his sons, Titus and Domitian, who had a hand in its construction. The irony is that its now universally accepted name, the Colosseum, probably refers to a colossal statue of the emperor Nero that stood by the building. Not that the many thousands of animals and humans who died in the amphitheatre when it was in use would have probably cared much about that.

The Bay of Naples and the End of Pompeii, AD 79

Life laughter and love
blossom beside turquoise foam
red petals above.

Pretty much everybody knows about Pompeii's spectacular and tragic end, destroyed by the eruption of Vesuvius. However, in some sense, the destruction of Pompeii is doubly tragic. This wasn't a place where catastrophe were supposed to take place. The Bay of Naples was Rome's party zone, where people came to play and laugh and have fun. It wasn't supposed to be a place of awful death and destruction. The area had seen fighting during Rome's wars with Hannibal and it had been involved in the rebellion of Spartacus, but under the Early Empire much of it had become a luxury playground for Rome's rich and famous, where they indulged theirs whims, including some of the more unusual ones. Tiberius had his villa on Capri where among other activities he is alleged to have recruited, for his secret orgies, teams of men and women who would conduct live threesome couplings, or perhaps that should be triplings. A wall painting in Pompeii depicts such activities. The lavishness of some of the villas at Pompeii shows how luxurious life could be for the wealthy. Caligula is even said to have built galleys with ten banks of oars and jewelled sterns in which he would cruise along the Campanian coast and enjoy the on-board baths, colonnades and banquet halls.

Roman Mosaics

Whole worlds in pieces
your feet walk in fantasies
the cunning hand moves.

Various cultures around the world have used mosaics at different times and in different forms. For many today, though, the fully glory of mosaics is most closely associated with Rome, and when archaeologists on a dig start turning up little square tesserae, they can usually be pretty sure they have a Roman site. Like so much of their culture the Romans borrowed the basic idea from the Greeks. The Greeks had started constructing designs on floors using natural pebbles before turning to deliberately cut pieces of marble and limestone. The Romans adopted this originally Greek art form with a passion. By the time Pompeii was destroyed its floors and walls were decorated with a wide range of mosaics, from the simple and utilitarian to amazing works like the Alexander Mosaic found in the House of the Faun showing a detailed, crowded battle scene as Alexander charges the Persian King Darius. Some early mosaics, like early TV, were in black and white, and the use of natural materials for tesserae limited the artists' palette (though less than you might think). However, the Romans soon started experimenting with glass tesserae for wall mosaics, giving their artists access to a whole new range of bright colours. And in the late Roman period glass tesserae involving gold leaf came into use, allowing the full glory of mosaics like those at Ravenna to shine forth.

Celebrity Actors

Life's a pantomime
and the tragedy often
is played out off stage.

Rome loved the theatre. It was perhaps, though, a little more ambivalent about actors, who were generally seen as not quite respectable. That said, actors, like modern movie stars, could become hugely rich and famous and mingle with the Roman elite. A pantomime actor called Mnester was, for instance, a favourite of the emperor Caligula. Caligula, as a serious fan, did not take kindly to anyone from the crowd who interrupted him and would flog them himself. Mnester subsequently became a favourite of the empress Messalina who wanted in addition a rather different type of performance from the handsome man. Mnester eventually ended up dead about the same time Messalina did, after a plot to remove Claudius failed. Nero himself, of course, loved to appear on stage. Later, in the 1st century, a talented and handsome Egyptian actor called Paris would catch the eye and enjoy the bed of Domitian's wife, the empress Domitia Longina. She ended up divorced. He ended up dead as well, with his grieving fans also threatened with death. As ever, mixing with the imperial family could bring great rewards, but it also brought enormous risks.

A Roman Fleet Reaches the Orkneys, AD 84

From centre sea to
ice blue, steel cold, north ocean
too far from Rome home.

The sheer extent and ambition of Roman military adventures can often come as a surprise. Even today, to many in the south of Britain, the Orkneys seem remote, situated in the cold seas to the north of mainland Scotland. At some time probably around 84, with Domitian, third emperor of the Flavian dynasty on the throne, a Roman fleet reached the Orkneys on a voyage linked to a failed Roman attempt to conquer Caledonia. It was not the first voyage involving men from the Mediterranean to reach northern seas. Centuries before, for instance, a Greek, Pytheas, had ventured north and wrote of sea ice and the midnight sun. However, the details of much what he did and where he went are still controversial. Tacitus writes that the Roman fleet landed and conquered the Orkneys. The reference to conquest, admittedly, might be an exaggeration. There is little other evidence for it. However, a few Roman items have been found on some sites on the islands and there seems little reason to doubt the word of Tacitus that a Roman fleet did make it that far, even though Rome's power would not endure in these northern waters.

The Conquest of Dacia, 101-106

Free Dacia attacked
death now decoration on
conqueror's column.

Rather better known these days as a car brand, Dacia is the name of an ancient region located in modern Romania. Much of the Roman Empire was under Roman control long before an emperor sat in Rome. Britain (at least the part that Rome ever controlled) was a late addition to the Empire. Dacia was to become an even later one and represents one of the high water marks of the Empire. By the end of the 1st century AD Romans and Dacians had a long a history of contact, some of it amicable, some of it hostile. During the reign of Domitian, last emperor of the Flavian dynasty, the Dacians attacked into Roman-controlled Moesia. In 96, Domitian's controversial rule was terminated by assassination and after the brief reign of Nerva Trajan became emperor in 98. In 101 he advanced north against the Dacians. By 102, Trajan had done sufficient damage to the forces and territory of the Dacian king Decebalus to force him to sign a peace allowing a Roman garrison in his capital, Sarmizegetusa. In 105 war broke out again and this time the Romans destroyed Sarmizegetusa, killed or expelled large numbers of civilians and drove Decebalus into the mountains and to killing himself. The Romans never occupied all of Dacia but in the area they did control they established the province of Dacia, and a column was erected in Rome to mark the conquest. Trajan's Column's spiral narrative cartoon is about as close to an original Roman war movie as we are ever going to get.

Trajan Reaches the Persian Gulf, 116

After such killing,
conquest, such travels, an end
but it is your own.

Trajan is a huge figure in the history of the Roman Empire, and in some ways, to many Romans, a model of what an emperor should be and could be. He was chosen as successor by Nerva, not because of blood ties or family prominence. He was from Spain and selected by Nerva for his talents. He had a quiet love life, he was comparatively careful with money, he did not randomly terrorise the inhabitants of the Empire, he put up big, impressive buildings and, perhaps above all, he conquered. However, even Trajan's career shows up some of the limitations of the Roman Empire. In 110, the Parthians had removed a pro-Roman monarch in Armenia, so a few years later Trajan decided to show them who was boss. He advanced east and in 115 he seized and annexed much of Mesopotamia and created a Roman province. But he wasn't finished. He advanced further and took Babylon and the Parthian capital at Ctesiphon near what is now Baghdad. He then pressed on until he reached the Persian Gulf. He was by then in his sixties. It is said that he looked eastwards over the Persian Gulf and wept, knowing he would never rival the conquests of Alexander the Great. He died a short time later in 117, and his successor Hadrian would withdraw west of the Euphrates.

Rome's Roads

No mere stone, gravel
alleys for life to love too
and war's red footsteps.

It is hardly going to be news to most people that the Romans built roads. Indeed it is one of the first aspects of the Roman Empire that tends to get mentioned if people are asked what they know about it. Having said that, the sheer scale of their achievement in this respect is sometimes underestimated. The Romans did not invent roads, but they did create a sophisticated network of roads right across the Empire, from the cold north to the burning desert, hundreds of thousands of miles of them, and tens of thousands of miles of these were actually hard-surfaced. Not only this but there were the other elements of the system that went with the roads themselves, like milestones and *mansiones*, accommodation for those travelling on official business. The network had a key military function, allowing troops to move rapidly around the Empire. However, it also revolutionised personal life and commercial life, helping the development of large-scale manufacturing operations distributing their products over wide areas. It did, however, from the point of view of the emperors also have some rather less positive effects. It inevitably allowed rebel troops to move quickly around the Empire. Once invaders from beyond the borders entered, they too could raid rapidly across the Empire.

Hadrian and Antinous

Rome's exile roaming
the empire, what did you gain?
We know you lost much.

Hadrian's approach to being emperor was markedly different from that of Trajan. Unlike Trajan's enthusiasm for conquest, Hadrian was more concerned with stabilising the Empire, even if that meant abandoning expansion plans. Hadrian's Wall is the best-known example of this, but it was an approach he pursued elsewhere. What he also pursued was travel. Some emperors rarely or never left Italy. Hadrian spent many years and large parts of his reign travelling the Empire, visiting provinces, inspecting military forces and making improvements and reforms. His motivation for such marathon journeys probably lay in a genuine desire to improve the Empire and leave a lasting legacy. His home life was not the happiest. In the year 100, with Trajan still ruling, he had married the emperor's grand-niece, Vibia Sabina. It was an important move in Hadrian's eventual succession to the throne and he remained married. The marriage, however, was not a hugely affectionate one. By contrast, in the late 120s he became very fond of a young Bithynian man called Antinous, who accompanied him on some of his journeys. In 130, while the imperial party was cruising on the Nile, Antinous seems to have drowned. Exactly how and why he died has been the subject of much speculation over the centuries. What is known is that Hadrian was grief-stricken, and being emperor he could express his grief how he chose. He ordered that Antinous be worshipped as a god across the Empire. A city called Antinopolis and temples were built. Statues of the young man were carved. Games were held in his honour.

The Bar Kokhba Rebellion, 132-135

Rebelling you made
Hadrian and Rome tremble.
You paid a grave price.

Hadrian spent a lot of time trying to understand the various regions of his empire. He clearly, however, did not take the trouble to understand the Jewish people. He seems to have decided that the area should be extensively Romanized. In 132, the Jews rose in rebellion again, this time under the leadership of Simeon Bar Kokhba. A Jewish state was again established and once more had some notable successes against the Romans. Legio XXII Deiotariana was severely mauled. Hadrian raced to crush the rebellion. In 134 he himself headed to the war and he also rushed massive reinforcements to the area together with his general from Britain, Julius Severus. Having assembled a huge army the Romans gradually began to destroy the revolution, advancing through the region. In the end Bar Kokhba was surrounded in the fortress of Betar. In 135 the fortress finally fell and the inhabitants were massacred. By the time the rebellion was finally crushed hundreds of thousands were dead, Judaea was devastated, many Jews had fled into exile and the access of Jews to Jerusalem was restricted. But the Romans had suffered heavily too. Hadrian declined a triumphal entry to Rome and in his report to the senate he left out the usual 'I and the Army are well.'

A Mountain of Amphora Sherds

So monumental
Rome that even its rubbish
becomes a mountain

Sometimes it's hard to understand the full scale of trade taking place across the Roman Empire while it was fully flourishing. In Rome, however, there is a mountain of evidence, literally. Rome has seven main hills at its heart. But it also has a small hill, Monte Testaccio, some 150 feet tall, made up almost entirely of broken amphorae. This amazing creation near the Tiber is the final resting place of amphorae which were used to transport olive oil from Spain and North Africa to the hungry mouths of the Empire's mother city. The olives were processed in their home countries, then the oil was put into the amphorae and they were transported by ship to Rome, where the oil was decanted and the amphorae discarded. It is estimated there are the remains of tens of millions of amphorae on the hill that were originally transported across the Mediterranean. It is powerful evidence of the size of just one of the types of large-scale trade that were taking place during the high point of the Empire.

Hair Fashions for Men

Short, long, straight, curly
shaven, bearded, harsh, relaxed
all are heirs of Rome.

People basing their views on TV and film drama, might think there was only one haircut for men in the Roman Empire, a sort of short back and sides that might also have been seen extensively on British streets in the 1940s and 1950s. In fact, over the centuries a wide variety of looks came into fashion and went out again. Then as now, celebs would play a role in moulding fashion. Whatever look the emperor chose would be seen on coins across the Empire. In the Republic a lot of Romans did go around with a rather severe short back and sides, but by the Early Empire, you could go for something a little softer, a little more like classical Greek perhaps, seen in the gentle, short curls of Augustus or Claudius. Nero, a man fiercely in love with Greek culture, would even go a little bouffant and add a hint of beard. Hadrian would go pretty much full Greek. By the late 2nd century, the beard of Marcus Aurelius might still have adorned some Greek philosopher, but his ebullient, bouffant curls were a striking and rather original look that had gone some distance beyond any Greek originals. A number of subsequent rulers, like Septimius Severus, were also keen on this look. They, however, were followed by soldier emperors who would bring back the short back and sides. The Tetrachs would take this to extremes with an almost shaved head, a number 1, like a 1960s US marine in boot camp, before Constantine once again went for a softer look with gentle curls, more like the early emperors.

The Roman Army

You are their sword but
how many emperors feel
your own fatal kiss?

One institution that was key to building the Empire, fighting civil wars over the Empire, and then trying to defend the Empire was, of course, the Roman Army. The core of the army was the legions. Made up of Roman citizens, each legion had something over 5,000 men in it, and for much of the the Empire's existence there were roughly around 30 legions. Legions could be moved around the Empire, depending on where they were needed and sometimes there were changes in the line-up. The disappearance of Legio IX Hispana from the records in the 2nd century has led to much speculation about how and why it disappeared. However, while the legions were the core of the army, Rome needed far more troops to defend its Empire, so it had also had the Auxiliaries, non-citizens who would acquire citizenship on discharge after completing their service. These came from a wide range of ethnic sources and many brought with them particular military skills from their homelands. In its prime and when well led, the imperial Roman army was a war machine of spectacular complexity, efficiency and logistical sophistication.

Famous Roman Horses

The Empire gallops,
even liveliest chargers
find death in the end

Many Romans, of course, loved their horses just as much as people do today, and famous race horses became particularly beloved. A mosaic from Constantine in North Africa shows a race horse with the inscription, 'Whether you win or don't win, we love you, Polidoxus.' The poet Horace lamented that despite his own popularity with the people of Rome and the nations of the Empire, the horse Andraemon was just as well known. Caligula, of course, famously loved the race horse Incitatus, lavishing luxury accommodation on the horse and infamously saying he would make it consul. If Caligula did say this, it's hard to know whether he was serious or joking but his enthusiasm for the horse seems real. Lucius Verus is said to have been hugely fond of the race horse Volucer that ran for the Green chariot team. He allegedly had a golden statue of the horse made and when Volucer died, Verus had a tomb made for him on the Vatican Hill. Hadrian was extremely fond of his favourite hunting horse, Borysthenes. When the horse died at Apte, Gallia Narbonensis, Hadrian had a tomb built for Borysthenes, too, with an inscription on it describing how the horse used to fly across the countryside after Pannonian boars.

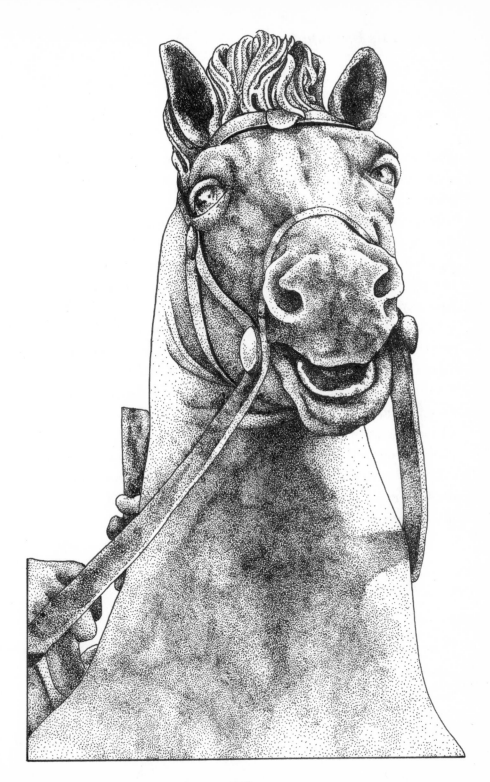

The *Classis Britannica*

Classic Classis old
British navy ploughs grey fields
the harvest is war.

The British navy has at various times and in various permutations played a major role through much of British history, but the first force to be named the British Fleet was created by Rome. Rome, of course, had military ships and fleets in the Mediterranean for most of its history, but the *Classis Britannica* was something else, a fleet that operated in the waters of Oceanus, the great, mysterious body of water that Romans thought of as surrounding the world. Roman naval ships are known to have played a significant role both in the initial invasion of Britain and in subsequent operations there, such as Agricola's invasion of Caledonia. At some point the naval units here were formalised as the *Classis Britannica*. Tiles stamped with the initials CL BR for *Classis Britannica* have been found at a number of locations linked with the fleet's operations including Dover, Folkestone, Lympne, Pevensey and, showing the trans-Channel function of the fleet, at Boulogne in France. The British fleet played a role in the story of Carausius and Allectus, and as seaborne raiders from across the North Sea increased their attacks on Britain in the 4th century, ships of the Roman forces based in Britain presumably played a significant role fighting against them.

The Antonine Wall

Rome's hopes of captive
Caledonia not concrete,
Firth and turf instead.

Hadrian's Wall is one of the best known Roman constructions anywhere in the world. However, in some sense a different wall in the north seems to sum up rather better the Roman experience in what is now Scotland. A few people make the mistake of assuming Hadrian's Wall runs along the border between England and Scotland. It does run close to the border at its western end, however, most of it is deep inside England. By contrast the Antonine Wall, originally built under Hadrian's successor, Antoninus Pius, marked another Roman attempt to advance into Caledonia and runs right through the Central Belt of Scotland from the Firth of Forth to the Firth of Clyde. If in some sense the stones of Hadrian's Wall suggest the longevity of the Roman presence in the north of Britain, then the largely turf and wood Antonine Wall (though formidable itself when first built) suggests the opposite. It was occupied at times but only ever briefly, before the Romans retreated south to more easily defended territory. Its remains, though still fascinating and substantial in places, are far less obvious than those of Hadrian's Wall.

Marcus Aurelius and his Meditations

Philosopher king,
wrote words to inspire himself
they still inspire others.

In 161 Antoninus Pius died and his two adopted sons, Marcus Aurelius and Lucius Verus, succeeded him as joint emperors. It was, by the Roman standards of the day, a very unusual arrangement and one which could have led to major problems long term. Verus, however, died in 169 leaving Marcus Aurelius sole emperor. Also unusually, for Roman emperors, Marcus Aurelius tends to be noted these days not for excesses of any kind, not for profligacy, but for a book. Marcus had become interested in philosophy as a youth, taking a particular interest in the works of the Greek Stoic, Epictetus. And when he came to write what are now known as The Meditations of Marcus Aurelius, he wrote in Greek. It is not certain he ever intended them to be published. They seem to be thoughts and reflections he wrote as much as anything for himself, while dealing with the job of being emperor as he saw it. It is an extraordinary insight into the mind of a Roman emperor at a key time in the Empire's development and elements of its Stoic philosophy, of dealing with life's struggles with as much positivity as possible, have inspired many over the centuries.

Roman Parties

We will laugh and live.
Until history catches
up with us, drink, sing.

The Romans liked a party. Obviously many parties were quite conservative affairs, and equally obviously, not everything written then about Roman celebrity parties was true. But some of it must have been. While Marcus Aurelius was studying philosophy, his co-emperor was allegedly having a rather more wild time with a party that cost six million sesterces and involved presenting each guest with gifts of the handsome slave who served them, live animals, gold and silver goblets and a carriage complete with mules and muleteers to take them home. The emperor Nero is said to have taken over a tank designed for gladiatorial sea fights for one of his parties where he was waited upon by prostitutes and dancing girls from all over Rome. The emperor Commodus pushed a fully clothed senator into a swimming pool and then had him dance naked in front of concubines. In the 3rd century the emperor Carus is said to have filled his palace with actors, prostitutes, pantomime artists and singers and conducted parties at which a hundred pounds of birds and fish and one thousand pounds of meat were served. Not all Roman imperial parties involved that kind of excess. On one occasion the emperor Domitian is reported to have amused himself by inviting guests to a banquet hall painted black, everything in it black, with gravestones next to each couch with the guest's name and other funeral kit. Naked serving boys painted black served the guests, who were left wondering which of them would actually be killed that night.

The Marcomanni and Qadi Attack, 169

Rome stands tall and proud
already men are at work
attacking your plinth.

For almost the first two centuries of its existence, the Roman Empire was, very broadly speaking, on the offensive. For the next three centuries it would be, very broadly speaking, on the defensive. By the 160s peoples were on the move beyond the borders of the Empire. In 161 the Parthians invaded Syria. Marcus Aurelius sent his co-emperor Lucius Verus, supported by some able generals, east to halt the enemy. The Romans had fought the Parthians before and this time they achieved a decisive victory. However, the returning troops brought home plague that killed millions. And more was to come. The Parthian threat was far from Rome and familiar. What happened next wasn't. After some comparatively minor Germanic raids had been dealt with, in around 169 Germanic Marcomanni and Qadi streamed across the Danube and eventually smashed a path into Italy itself and besieged Aquileia, one of the major Roman cities in northern Italy. Marcus Aurelius put a range of emergency measures into operation and eventually managed to push the invaders out of Italy. The Romans now launched attacks into the territory of the Marcomanni and the Qadi. The campaigns against Germanic and Sarmatian tribes that would occupy Marcus Aurelius for much of the rest of his life were successful for him and for Rome, and the Column of Marcus Aurelius in Rome, a lesser known version of Trajan's Column, celebrates his victories. The wars, however, were brutal. One scene shows Roman soldiers destroying a village and terrorising civilians. And the invasions were, without doubt, a sign of what was to come.

Commodus and Death in the Arena, 177-192

Comedy rule kills,
the arena of your dreams
becomes a nightmare.

Commodus was not one of Rome's best emperors. Very far from it. However, he has gained a particular place in modern culture due to his appearance in the movie *Gladiator*. For those who have not seen the film, let's just say he is definitely not the hero of the piece. Commodus was the son of Marcus Aurelius but by no means a chip off the old block. Commodus was made co-emperor at the age of 17. He spent time with his father as Marcus Aurelius campaigned on the Danube front, but soon after his father died in March 180 Commodus made peace and returned home. In 182, his sister Lucilla became involved in a plot to kill him. The plot failed but it would be the first of a number of plots against him. The actions of Commodus became more eccentric, as the possession of absolute power helped destabilise him. He renamed Rome after himself and the months of the year after his names and titles. Stories abounded of sexual antics, like watching some of his many concubines have sex with others. And, of course, he fought in the arena. Or at least he killed in the arena. From a platform he slaughtered animals, including decapitating ostriches with crescent-headed arrows. He fought gladiators who let him win because he was the Emperor and in return he would only wound them. He killed weaker men who couldn't defend themselves. He dressed as Hercules with club and skin. In the end, conspirators had a wrestler strangle him in December 192.

Roman Coins

They bought good, bought bad
now across the centuries
their voices speak still.

Vast numbers of coins were produced bearing the heads of emperors and other key members of the imperial family. They still turn up in large quantities within what was the Empire, and in smaller numbers they turn up far beyond the boundaries of the Empire. Roman coins have, for instance, been found in Scandinavia and Sri Lanka. They are hugely valued by archaeologists because the name of the emperor or imperial family member they carry, and other information on them, often allows them to be dated quite precisely, which in turn helps date the context in which they are found. Many collectors appreciate the designs on them and the sheer thrill of holding something so old. Coins were, of course, hugely important to the Romans themselves. Some provincial towns minted their own coins, but the main Roman coinage was a single currency that helped commercially unite a huge number of different peoples and cultures within the Empire. And coins were the party political broadcasts of their day. On one side they showed the name and face of the emperor (very important when the occupier of the imperial throne might change regularly). On the other they carried a message in words and pictures. This could be something general like a reference to Rome or it could be much more specific, like announcing a particular imperial victory. And if, as an emperor, you were worried about civil war breaking out, then why not have a lot of coins minted proclaiming how peaceful your empire was and how loyal your troops were?

Gods from the East

Religions head west.
One God will change Rome's empire
in many senses.

From early on, Romans had supplemented their belief in the combination of Italian and Greek deities that was the foundation of Roman religion with religions imported from the east. The worship of Cybele and Bacchus had both been introduced more than a century and half before the end of the Republic. Isis and Serapis also became established deities in Rome. Christianity arrived in Rome from the Middle East in the 1st century AD. The cult of Mithras, particularly popular with the military and inspired originally by some religious ideas from Persia, arrived in Rome about the same time. In later centuries the cult of the sun became an important religion in Rome. 'Sol Invictus' the 'Unconquered Sun' appeared on Constantine's coins before he became a Christian. Often these new religions sat comfortably side by side with the traditional Roman religion. Sometimes they did not. The emperor Elagabalus, priest of the Emesan sun god before becoming emperor, surprised Rome by marrying the Vestal Virgin Aquilia Severa. Judaism and Christianity caused particular problems for the Roman authorities because of their adherents' determined rejection of all other religions as false.

Didius Julianus and the Empire Auction, 193

You buy the empire
for cold cash, the final price
is colder your life.

In the late 2nd century and in the 3rd century, as the battle for imperial power became a free for all, emperors arrived on the imperial path by many routes. For most the cold steel of their men was their ticket to (often brief) occupation of the imperial throne. For Didius Julianus though, it was cold hard cash. Julianus came from a leading family in Mediolanum (Milan) and had had a military and political career. He might conceivably have become emperor by more conventional means. However, when in June 193 the Praetorian Guard murdered the emperor Pertinax, successor to Commodus, they decided to make themselves rich by auctioning the Empire. Julianus found himself in a bidding war against Titus Flavius Sulpicianus, father of Pertinax's wife. In the end Julianus won with a bid of the massive amount of 25,000 sesterces to be paid to each of the guard. Julianus the winner was, however, ultimately the loser. It turned out that even in late 2nd century Rome, there were maybe some limits to what a man could acceptably do to win the throne. Demonstrators called for the army to get involved and across the Empire a number of generals saw their opportunity. After a reign of just over two months, the Danube legions arrived in Italy and Julianus was killed.

Battle of the African Emperors, 197

African lions
grip empire in talons, teeth.
Many will be clawed.

On 19 February 197, a ferocious battle took place at Lugdunum, Lyon, in Gaul, between two men determined to rule the Roman world. Both were African emperors. By 197, the North African coastline had been controlled by Rome for a very long time. A hybrid culture had grown up along the African coast west of Egypt that mixed indigenous Africans with the descendants of Phoenicians, Carthaginians and Greeks and with Romans, producing both families and a civilisation with a diverse heritage. This civilisation built beautiful cities, the ruins of which still amaze today. And it produced ambitious, talented people. Septimius Severus was born in Lepcis Magna in what is now Libya. After a distinguished career his legions advanced on Rome and with Didius Julianus dead, he took over there. In his efforts to seize the throne, Severus had an ally, the governor in Britain Clodius Albinus, also from North Africa, also with a distinguished career, also with imperial ambitions. Severus recruited him as his deputy and heir, his Caesar, until he had dealt with another rival Pescennius Niger. Having dealt with that threat though, Severus made his son Caesar. Albinus declared himself emperor and invaded Gaul. The two armies met in the fiercest and perhaps largest battle ever between Roman forces. After initial success, the forces of Albinus were eventually routed and Albinus ended up with his head cut off. The victor established a new dynasty, the Severan dynasty, which would last a few decades before the chaos of the 3rd century really began.

Roman Baths and Being Roman

The undressed truth of
Rome's baths. It is not for some.
Hot, wet and steamy.

Rome didn't only export violence and exploitation to the world. Like all successful empires it also attempted with some success to export shared values. Some of these were cultural, some of these were concrete, or at least, bricks and concrete. Across the Empire many ambitious locals keen to seem more Roman, along with those who just fancied some Roman luxury, adopted elements of Roman life including, of course, Roman baths. The basic concept was a suite of changing rooms, with warm, hot and cold rooms in the baths area, where the user would warm up, sweat and clean up. It must have been quite an experience for those used to more simple bathing arrangements. Roman bathing establishments ranged in size from the tiny to the vast and magnificent like the Baths of Caracalla in Rome. People went there to get clean, to do business and to have fun - sometimes too much fun for Roman moralists. Mixed naked bathing was at times common despite disapproval by some. The Suburban Baths at Pompeii, which only have one changing room, presumably used by both men and women, also have a series of distinctly racy frescoes depicting a variety of activities including group sex – not the kind of wall decoration you tend to see at suburban baths these days. An early Byzantine writer tells of a 'lustful nun' of Alexandria who used to tour bath houses tempting laymen and even clerics into sex acts with her. It would be fair to say Clement of Alexandria was not a fan of the wealthy noblewomen he describes showing off their naked bodies to men amidst the gold and silver luxury of the baths.

The *Limes*

Rome's ambition knows
no limits, but this empire
must still have borders.

In Britain, particularly, when we think of a Roman border, *limes*, we tend
to think of Hadrian's Wall. It looks like what a hard Roman border should,
with its stone walls, forts and outposts. It is, however, only 73 miles long.
The Roman Empire, for most of its existence had borders that ran right
across Europe, a huge distance through Asia and then across Africa. They
weren't protected like Hadrian's Wall, but where there were no strong
natural barriers, the borders were given protection. Generally speaking
the Roman frontiers were defended by carefully arranged systems of
forts and watchtowers, with occasional uses of palisades and ditches at
areas of particular strategic significance. Roads were vital to allow rapid
movement of troops to respond to threats against the frontier. Major
rivers were excellent border defences. In the east, Rome relied greatly on
the Euphrates as a border for long periods, though it also again built forts
and roads that ran for hundreds of miles along the edge of the desert. In
Africa, the formidable Sahara Desert was the natural frontier in many
places, but forts were still built and the spectacular Fossatum Africae,
a linear defensive structure similar in some ways to Hadrian's Wall but
much longer, defended the ancient core of Roman-controlled Africa in
what is now Tunisia and eastern Algeria. No borders this long though
could ever be totally secure and despite Rome's efforts, they would be
breached many times in the 3rd, 4th and 5th centuries.

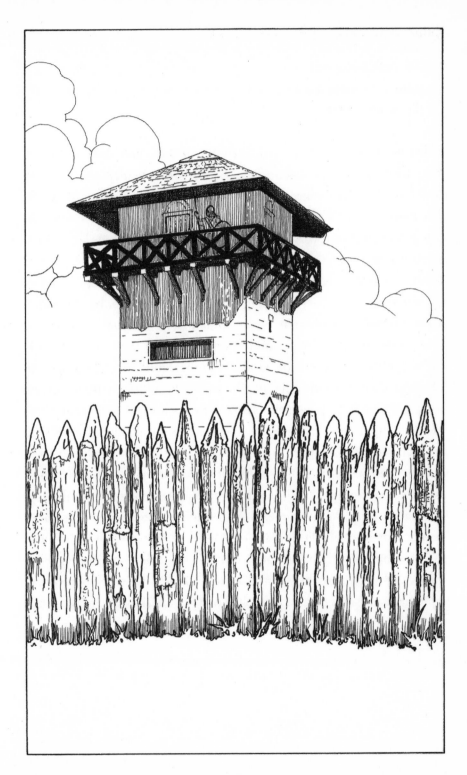

Spices and India, Silk and China

The East unconquered
roars round the world defiant
gobbles Roman gold.

When we discuss the history of early European colonialism in Asia in the 16th, 17th and 18th centuries, there is still a tendency to think of Europeans venturing into areas totally unknown to the west. However, this ignores the fact that the Romans, even though they could not conquer them, were very well aware of places like China and India, and quite extensive trade networks linked the Roman Empire to both. Trade networks linking China and India to the west were, of course, not new even then. They had long existed and Alexander of Macedon's invasions had taken him as far as Afghanistan and India. Inevitably, Rome's increasing affluence and fascination with the rare and exotic led to a huge increase in demand for luxury goods such as silk from China and spices from India. In the 1st century Pliny the Elder would complain that Roman women's demand for eastern luxuries was costing 100 million sesterces a year. Some of this trade was conducted over land through Asian middlemen, some of it came direct across the sea from India to Red Sea ports in Egypt. And it wasn't just goods comparatively easily transported in small quantities that were brought from the east to Rome. Tigers, for example, were brought to appear in gladiatorial games. A mosaic at Villa Romana del Casale at Piazza Armerina in Sicily shows a capture tiger being handled by Roman soldiers in the early 4th century. Direct contact between Rome and China was limited but Roman diplomatic missions may have reached there in the 2nd and 3rd centuries.

The Edict of Caracalla, 212

Too late made equals
so equally to endure
western empire's end.

Caracalla was not this emperor's official name. He was the son of Septimius Severus and Julia Domna, officially known by various other less remarkable names. He is, however, known to history by the nickname Caracalla he got from being fond of a particular type of cloak. He is notable for looking exceptionally cross in some of his imperial portraits. Considering the amount of fury that blew through the imperial household over the centuries, it's quite an achievement to look even more cross than other emperors. He did not have a glittering career on the imperial throne, but he is still well-known for his 212 Edict, or *Constitutio Antoninana* (from his official name). In it he gave all freeborn inhabitants of the Empire Roman citizenship. Many have looked for cynical motives in this move. One Roman historian suggested he was looking to expand the tax base. However, it is worth pointing out that Caracalla himself was the son of an African father and a Syrian mother. Perhaps he just felt it was right that everybody in Syria and Roman-controlled Africa and elsewhere in the Empire should finally be able to call themselves 'Citizen'.

The Four Julias

Female dynasty
for four Julias come joined
on history's throne.

We are used to thinking of male dynasties in the Roman imperial family, not so used to thinking of dynasties of women. However, at the end of 2nd century and beginning of the 3rd, four women, all called Julia and all linked by blood played a major role in the imperial family and in the Empire itself. All had coins minted in their name. Julia Domna, the first of these remarkable, influential, powerful women was born in Emesa in Syria and married the ambitious, talented Septimius Severus. When he became emperor, she accompanied him on many of his journeys and she bore him two sons. Both Caracalla and Geta would become emperors. When they had both been assassinated she killed herself. After her death she was worshipped. Julia Domna's elder sister, Julia Maesa, had two daughters, Julia Soaemias and Julia Mamaea. Julia Maesa plotted to put the son of Julia Soaemias on the throne claiming he was the son of Caracalla. Between them these two Julias succeeded in making the teenager, who would become known as Elagabalus, the emperor. They had great influence over him. When Elagabalus fell, his mother was killed with him. When she could see the reign of Elagabalus becoming unpopular, Julia Maesa switched her support to the young son of Julia Mamaea. The two women between them would then make him emperor as Severus Alexander. Julia Maesa would die during his reign and be worshipped after her death. In 235 Julia Mamaea was murdered along with Severus Alexander by rebellious troops.

Elagabalus, Teen Emperor, 218-222

Sun son you are far
too much for Rome you set soon
in the dark Tiber.

The joy and the curse of being emperor was that you pretty much could do anything you liked. The lives of the Roman emperors are interesting experiments in what men might do if there were no controls on them. And not just men, teenagers too. The emperor now generally known to history as Elagabalus was the son of Julia Soemias. In 217, Caracalla, successor to Septimius Severus, was murdered and soon after troops in Syria where Elagabalus was growing up proclaimed him the son of Caracalla and emperor. Soon this young teenager who had been growing up in Emesa (now Homs) as high priest of the Syrian sun god by whose name he is now known, was headed for Rome. It was going to be a shock for the city. Elagabalus was an unconventional young man by Roman standards. He gave his Syrian god pride of place in Rome. He married a string of women, including a vestal virgin. According to Roman sources he also danced and dressed like a woman, and propositioned men in brothels. He had as his 'husband' a charioteer called Hierocles and it is claimed that he offered surgeons large sums of money if they could create an artificial vagina for him. It is hard to know now how much truth there is in the stories. It may simply have been that the Romans were unable to come to terms with having as their emperor a young Syrian priest with a passion for new experiences. In the end the Praetorian Guard had had enough, murdered him and dumped his body in the Tiber.

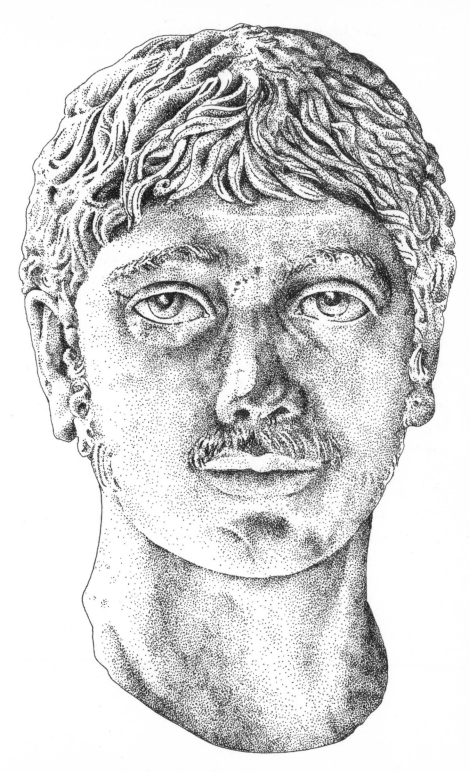

Maximinus Thrax and the Year of the Six Emperors, 238

Six stride on the sand
in the arena of thrones
only one escapes.

Pretty much from the start of the Empire, holding the imperial seat had been an exercise in naked power backed by the threat of violence, but it was one usually covered in the raiment of Roman tradition and respectability. The young emperor Severus Alexander was in many respects a typical example of that, the last member of the Severan dynasty founded by Septimius Severus and his legions in 193, and by 235 in power for over four decades. What, and who, was to follow was very different. When the young, fresh-faced Alexander was assassinated in that year, the legions chose instead the grizzled, grim-faced Maximinus Thrax. Thrax sounds an almost sci-fi name, but in fact just means 'the Thracian'. He was a man with no family heritage of power and wealth whatsoever, the first to rise right through the ranks to military commander and then emperor. The following decades would be a bumpy ride for the Empire. The following years would be a bumpy ride for Maximinus. He fought invading tribes on the Danube and Rhine frontiers with some success. He was less successful against internal enemies. In 238 a succession of rebel emperors, Gordian I and II, Pupienus and Balbinus, and Gordian III rose against him with senate support. By the end of 238, five - including Maximinus, killed by his own troops - were dead, and Gordian III was emperor. For a while at least.

Philip the Arab and Rome's Millennium, 248

Little Rome has come
far in thousand years, Philip,
your journey ends soon.

Showing how diverse the contenders for the imperial throne were becoming, in 244 an emperor arrived on it who is officially known as Philip I, but has tended to be known in history as Philip the Arab or Philip the Arabian. He was born in a village not far from Damascus, which after he became emperor he remodelled and renamed, rather unimaginitively, Philippopolis, the city of Philip. By the time of the death of his predecessor Gordian III (in which Philip may or may not have had a hand) while campaigning against the Persians, Philip was praetorian prefect. Acclaimed emperor he managed to negotiate a peace with the Persians and extract Roman forces from a difficult situation. It wasn't going to get much easier for the Empire under Philip, as invaders now began to threaten the Danube frontier. Philip's reign did, however, see one fascinating landmark event. In 248, based on traditional dates, Rome celebrated its 1,000th anniversary with massive celebrations. The Christian writer Eusebius in the early 4th century claimed that Philip was a Christian, though there is little other evidence for this. In the end Philip made the mistake of sending one Trajan Decius to restore order on the Danube. Decius instead got himself elected emperor by the troops and marched south. Philip was defeated and killed near Verona.

The Death of Trajan Decius, 251

Rome's hopes, empire's fame,
eagles blood-stained and mud-stained
sunk in Cniva's swamp.

Philip I had not had a great reign. Nor did Trajan Decius. He bears the name of one of the most successful of Roman emperors, Trajan, but names can be misleading. In his portraits he tends to have a rather haggard and agonised look. Considering what happened to him in the end, it seems appropriate. Decius and his probably aristocratic wife Herennia Etruscilla seem to have been well in with the senate, and Decius seems to have made some efforts to boost traditional Roman politics, like a failed attempt to reintroduce the office of Censor as an independent role. He also issued an edict designed to boost traditional Roman attitudes commanding everyone to offer a sacrifice for the safety of the Empire. This, whether by design or not, led to the persecution of Christians who refused to make the sacrifice on religious grounds. And then there were the Goths. The Goths were to play a huge role in the disintegration of the Roman Empire. Decius was the first Roman emperor to experience fully, personally, what their arrival on the scene could mean. The Goths under their king Cniva crossed the Danube and raided deep into Roman-controlled territory plundering as they went. Decius with his army met the Goths in swampy ground in what is now Bulgaria. The Battle of Abritus in 251 was a disaster for Rome and for Decius. His son was killed early in the battle, the Goths managed to surround the Roman army and Decius and most of his men were slaughtered.

The Emperor Valerian Captured by Persians, 260

An emperor is
forced to kiss defeat's dry dust
Rome itself humbled.

People in Western Europe today perhaps inevitably tend to be more aware of Rome's battles with tribes on the Empire's European frontiers. They are less aware of the enemies Rome so frequently fought on its eastern frontier, the Parthians and then the Sassanian Persians. Modern European powers have often had a tough time in the region and so too did Rome. Licinius Valerianus had had a long political and military career before, in 253, he was acclaimed emperor by his troops. Perhaps he should have turned the offer down. A few years after he came to power, Frankish invaders had managed to cross Gaul into Spain, his son was fighting Alemmani invaders in northern Italy, there was rebellion in the Balkans, and Valerian himself was proving himself spectacularly unsuccessful in the east. At the Battle of Edessa in 260 in what is now southern Turkey, he managed to get himself not just defeated by the Sassanian King Shapur I, but captured as well. Rome had had some pretty useless emperors already, and the death of Decius at Abritus had taken place less than ten years earlier, but having an emperor actually surrender to a foreign enemy was a shock the Empire had never experienced before. What exactly happened to Valerian after his capture is not clear, but he never returned to what had been his empire and a famous rock carving at Naqsh-E Rostam in Iran shows him bowing in submission before the Persian king.

Postumus and the Gallic Empire

Northern and Gallic
gallantry prospers apart.
Rome's vengeance is near.

It is easy to make assumptions about history based in retrospect on what we know actually happened. We tend to assume, because it did, that the Roman Empire would remain largely intact as an entity – except for the division between the Western and Eastern Roman Empires – until almost the end in the West. Over the centuries, of course, such an assumption did not by any means appear valid all the time. In 260, it wasn't looking good for Rome in the west. Some Germanic invaders had made it as far as Spain and destroyed Tarragona, while the emperor Gallienus battled invaders at Milan. And it was in this year that a huge chunk of the Western Roman Empire temporarily defected from central control. A Roman commander probably born somewhere in north-west Europe, one Marcus Cassianius Latinius Postumus, defeated a band of roving invaders. When Saloninus the son of Gallienus tried to take control of the invaders' booty to decide what happened to it, Postumus was declared emperor by his troops and Saloninus rapidly ended up dead. Conventionally, Postumus might now have tried to seize Italy and Rome. Instead he settled for ruling Britain, Gaul, Spain and parts of Germany. He was a north European and he had created a largely northern European 'Roman' Empire which now tends to be called the Gallic Empire. Postumus would be killed by his own troops in 268 but his separate empire would last until the defeat of Tetricus by Aurelian in 274.

Claudius Gothicus and the Sea Invasion

They thrust a spear deep
into Rome's outer shield rim
Claudius holds firm.

Claudius II, or Claudius Gothicus as he tends to be known to history, for reasons that will become obvious, was another third-century emperor with a short imperial career. His reign is notable for another encounter with a huge Gothic invasion force, a rather more successful encounter for Rome than that of Trajan Decius. Details are fairly scarce but in 269 Claudius faced a massive dual threat in the Balkans. Hundreds of thousands of Goths invaded the Balkans on foot, but the Empire was also threatened by a fleet of, allegedly, 2000 ships that attacked Black Sea cities on the Empire's coast. They erupted into the Aegean and attacked targets there including Thessalonica. The exact make-up of the assorted invaders is not clear. One source gives a long list that includes Celts and Scythians, but also includes names more associated with the Goths: Greuthingi, Austrogothi, Tervingi, Visi. Such lists do probably say something about the mixed make-up of such mass migrations, but generally the Romans seem to have seen the Goths as the main element they faced. The fighting culminated in the Battle of Naissus near the city of Nis in southern Serbia. The Roman forces decisively defeated the invaders, killing perhaps 50,000 of them and capturing vast numbers of prisoners. The war was brutal and merciless, but Claudius Gothicus had held the line. For now.

Marius and the Sword, 269

Big name little reign
and short sharp cut to power
did your sword end it?

If you ask people to come up with a Roman called Marius, many will cite the general and seven-time consul who battled with Sulla for control of the late Republic. But the Roman Empire, or at least, the Gallic Empire, also had an emperor called Marius. He is not a historical figure on the scale of the Marius of the Republic. His full name was Marcus Aurelius Marius (and no, he was not a patch on Marcus Aurelius either). In 269 Postumus refused to allow his troops to sack Moguntiacum (Mainz). The troops decided that if Postumus wouldn't let them, they'd find somebody who would, so Postumus was killed and in his place they made Marius, an officer who it is said had once been a blacksmith, emperor. His rule was not to be long and glorious. Indeed it was neither long nor glorious. Life as an emperor in the turbulent third century could be very short indeed. A few days or weeks after he was made emperor he, too, was killed. He was perhaps a more successful blacksmith than emperor. It is said he was killed by a sword that he himself had manufactured. By contrast, his successor, Victorinus, who didn't last much longer as emperor either, was allegedly killed by a clerk whose wife he had slept with.

Gold and Silver, the Worth of an Empire

Hills of gold, mountains
of silver gleam, the future
will prove base metal.

Precious metals were at the heart of the Roman coinage in the Early Empire. The golden aureus and the silver denarius were the cornerstones of the system. Base metal coins like the sestertius and the bronze as were useful for smaller transactions, but the aureus and the denarius were familiar, predictable coins from one emperor to the next. Wars of conquest brought in some precious metals, but under the late Republic and the Early Empire, vast quantities of precious metals were also being mined, particularly in places like the Iberian peninsula. According to Pliny the Elder, mines in Lusitania, Asturia and Gallaecia produced 20,000 Roman pounds of gold every month. In the 3rd century though, with civil war and invasions from beyond the Empire's borders both disrupting the economy and demanding massive defence expenditure, emperors needed to make their precious metals go further, so the precious metal content of coinage was reduced until the silver coinage was essentially a bronze coinage. Under the Tetrarchs and the dynasty of Constantine some stability would be restored to the coinage and precious metal coins had a resurgence. However, as the security situation deteriorated in the 5th century, the Roman government would find itself paying vast amounts of precious metals to keep invaders temporarily quiet. And in Britain, as central Roman control collapsed, the locals would take to shaving silver off the edges of silver coins, something highly illegal under the Empire, to produce coins that theoretically had the same value but also allowed you to pocket some spare silver.

Zenobia, Queen of the East

Eastern desert storm
Rome's pal under you its mire
you hit like lightning.

Zenobia is one of the most extraordinary characters to appear on Roman coins and she wasn't even Roman. Her full name in its Romanised form was Septimia Zenobia, but she was in fact from Palmyra, that amazing city that was in the news recently during the fighting in Syria, or to be more precise she was Queen of Palmyra. After Valerian's defeat and capture by the Persians in 260, her husband Odaenathus, who had close ties with Rome, had played a key role, his forces preventing the Persians overrunning Rome's eastern provinces. In 267 or 268 Odaenathus was assassinated and Vaballathus, the young son of Odaenathus and Zenobia, became king. The real power though would be Zenobia, regent and queen. Whereas Odaenathus had been content to rule what was in reality a Palmyrene Empire, while still carefully pretending to accept Roman authority in the east, Zenobia would prove much more daring. With the Roman emperor of the time Claudius II battling Germanic invaders in Europe, Zenobia was free to cement Palmyrene power in the east. Then she went a whole lot further and seized Egypt and much of what is now Turkey. The Palmyrene Empire now stretched in a crescent around the shores of the eastern Mediterranean. Soon she was minting Roman coinage with her face on it and the legend ZENOBIA AUG, Zenobia Empress. It was all too much for the new emperor by then in power in Rome. Aurelian abandoned his problems in Europe and headed east. After some bitter fighting he finally managed to smash Zenobia's forces and capture the queen. How she finally died is unclear.

The End of Roman Dacia

Hills plain land complex
once Roman, Rome's home no more
first chip in the wall.

Amidst all the tumultuous events of the 3rd century, it is easy to ignore one that at the time may not have seemed hugely significant, but that in retrospect perhaps marks the beginning of the end of the Empire in Europe. Sometime in the 270s, Dacia, the capture of which had been something of a high water mark of the Roman Empire in Europe, ceased to be Roman-controlled. Trajan's Dacia disappears from maps of the Empire. Roman Dacia had for some time been under increasing pressure from Germanic tribes pressing west and south. In the end emperor Aurelian, facing major crises both in the west and the east, would be forced to pull the plug. He defiantly minted a coin with the reverse legend *Dacia Felix*, 'Happy Dacia', but Happy Dacia would in reality disappear. He pulled Roman citizens out of Dacia and established a new 'Dacia' in what had been Moesia. Constantine would later campaign in what had been Trajan's Dacia, but in the 270s the Roman Empire in Europe had taken a clear step backwards.

Saturnalia

Even empires need
holidays sometimes, less blood
more booze, fun, feast, food.

With its carols and cribs and nativity plays, and the name itself, Christmas is of course a Christian festival. However, if you look at the non-Christian elements of our Christmas, the celebration doesn't look that different from the festive season of the Romans, the Saturnalia. The Saturnalia was a Roman festival in honour of the god Saturn that came to be celebrated around the time of the Winter Solstice in December. It involved lots of drinking and feasting, and giving of gifts. It was a time of goodwill, when the wealthy might help out the poor and masters and slaves might briefly swap clothes and, on some level, positions. Public Saturnalia banquets and festivities were put on. The increasing popularity of the cult of Sol Invictus, the Unconquered Sun, in the 3rd century added another element to Roman winter festivities. As a Sun deity, the Winter Solstice was inevitably important to the cult's followers. In a Roman calendar for 354 there is even mention of a holiday for Invictus on 25th December. The only evidence for Jesus being born on December 25th is the assertion of that date as Christmas some time during the Roman period. However, who decided on that date, and when it was decided on, and on what evidence it was decided, is not clear. There has been, however, much speculation that how we choose to enjoy ourselves at Christmas, how we choose to make our festive season festive, has been influenced in some aspects by Saturnalia and various pagan Winter Solstice festivals.

Tetrarchs, the *Domini*

The dominant four
masters of empire for sure
soon the cracks will show.

By the death of the emperor Carus in 284 the third century had been a pretty turbulent time for the Empire. Something major was going to have change. Diocletian, a tough soldier probably from near Split in what is now Croatia, had become commander of the household cavalry under Carus. When Carus died while fighting the Persians, and his son Numerian died soon after, the army acclaimed Diocletian emperor. For a while, the other son of Carus, Carinus, was still alive in the west and claiming to be emperor too. After a battle with the forces of Diocletian near Belgrade he was neither. Diocletian was now sole emperor. He was determined to stabilise and strengthen both empire and the very office of emperor. During his reign, the face-saving pretence established by Augustus that it was the Senate who still ran the Empire, began to be abandoned. Eventually, the letters DN for *Dominus Noster*, 'Our Master' would appear on the coins of Roman emperors. The pretence was gone. He also established the Tetrarchy, from the Greek for 'rule by four.' It was a formal acknowledgement that the Empire was often too big and complex with too many threats to it to be ruled successfully by even two men. In 286 he made one of his fellow-soldiers, Maximian, his co-emperor, or Augustus. Diocletian would retain control of the east, Maximian would take the west. In 293 Constantius was made Caesar or deputy emperor and heir to Maximian in the west and Galerius was made Diocletian's Caesar in the east. Both Caesars then married into the families of their senior emperors.

Carausius and Allectus

First British Empire
the sun sets in crimson waves
a cloud of dark ships.

Marcus Aurelius Mauseus Carausius was born perhaps somewhere near the coast in what is modern Belgium. By 286 he was a senior Roman military commander and he was given the job by the Western emperor Maximian of commanding a fleet to clear Frankish and Saxon raiders off the sea. This he did with some success. However, a dispute developed over how Carausius operated and his attitude to booty recovered from the pirates. Maximian consequently ordered his execution. Carsusius decided he would instead rather rebel and seize, together with territory round the naval base at Gesoricaum, Boulogne, control of all of Britain. This he did. Maximian built a fleet with which to attack Carausius but the fleet was destroyed by a storm. Carausius successfully built for himself a little British Empire, minting coins in his name, some with cheery messages about Britain on them, and some even cheekily featuring Maximian and Diocletian, as if he and they were partners and equals. In 293 Maximian sent his Caesar Constantius to attack Carausius. Gesoriacum fell and Carausius was killed by his assistant Allectus, who then became, briefly, the next emperor of this British Empire. In 296, Constantius, along with his praetorian prefect, invaded Britain. Allectus gave battle but was defeated and killed.

Roman Bikinis

What is old is new
And suddenly centuries
may matter no more.

One of the fascinations of the Roman Empire is that to modern people it can seem at the same time both very strange and very familiar. The modern bikini was born in the post-World War 2 era, as women looked to cast off the restrictions of earlier generations and it took its explosive name from Bikini Atoll – a tropical island it is true, but one largely known at the time as place where the US tried out nuclear weapons. However, the Romans had bikinis too, though probably rather more for sports and dancing and for acrobats than for swimming. One of the amazing early 4th-century mosaics, from about the time of the Tetrachy, at Villa Romana del Casale at Piazza Armerina in Sicily, shows young women exercising in what today we would instantly recognise as bikinis. (Judging by the mosaics, the owner of this villa seems to have been a fan of good-looking women in skimpy costumes, and of sport, particularly hunting). The bikini bottoms shown in this mosaic are by today's standards rather of the 'big knickers' variety. However, a leather example found preserved in waterlogged levels from Roman London has a remarkably modern cut and even has ties at the side like many modern examples.

Roman Pets

Roman pet passion
even man-eating empires
have cute cuddly side.

Considering the thousands of animals slaughtered for public 'entertainment' in the amphitheatres of the Empire, it might be thought that the Romans were not that fond of animals. In reality many Romans loved their pets just as much as modern pet-owners. Dogs were hugely popular pets. Well-off ladies loved their lap dogs, and Juvenal writes of women who were a lot more fond of their lapdogs than their husbands. The emperor Tiberius had a pet snake. Birds also were kept by many. Some had parrots they taught to speak. Some of the rich kept peacocks. Cats seem to have been rather less popular with the Romans than they are today, but there were, of course, sacred cats in Egypt in pre-Christian times and cats seem to have become somewhat more popular in the late Roman period. Along with more everyday animals, the emperors, being emperors, kept some rather exotic ones as well. Caracalla had a lion that ate with him. The late Roman emperor Valentinian had two she-bears who lived in cages close to where he slept. One was called Gold Flake, the other, Innocence.

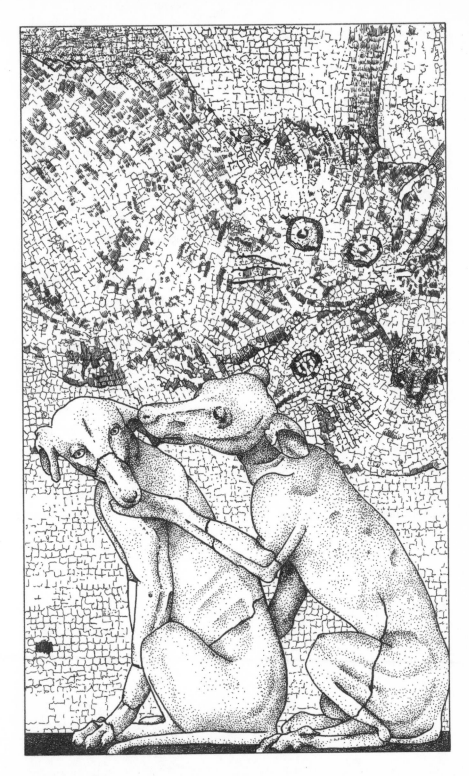

Diocletian Retires, 305

Weary he lays down
life's work, carefully watches
it crumbles to dust.

A key part of the Emperor Diocletian's ideas for the imperial administration was to avoid devastating battles for succession by ensuring a smooth hand-over of power. By creating the system of two Augusti, senior emperors, with two Caesars, deputy emperors, he had already established a clear official line of succession. In 305 he made another bold step. He abdicated, handing over his power to his Caesar, Constantius. Not only did he do this, but he got his fellow-emperor Maximian to retire too, handing over to Galerius. Two new Caesars, Severus in the west, and Maximinus in the east, were selected to serve as deputies to the two new senior emperors. Diocletian retired to his glorious and massive palace, which now forms about half the old town of the beautiful Croatian port city of Split. He presumably hoped that the Tetrarchic system would continue to run smoothly without him. It didn't. By the time he died in 316, it had fallen apart almost entirely as bloodlines reasserted themselves. In July 306 Constantius died at York. Ignoring the line of Tetrarchic succession, the troops of Constantius declared his son Constantine emperor. Later the same year, Maxentius, son of Maximian, was acclaimed emperor and his father Maximian once again became involved in imperial politics. Galerius sent his Caesar Severus to crush the rebellion, but Severus was crushed instead. Two years after he had retired, Diocletian's tetrarchic system was in chaos.

Constantine's Victory at the Milvian Bridge, 312

A bridge arches to
the future one victor will
Cross in triumph.

Six years after being acclaimed emperor by the troops of his deceased father and after years of imperial infighting, Constantine stood with an army outside Rome preparing to fight the army of Maxentius. What exactly went on in Constantine's head the night before the battle nobody knows, but it would later become tradition that Constantine came to think belief in Christ and the cross would give him victory. On 28 October 312, Constantine's forces smashed those of Maxentius. A collapsing pontoon bridge led to many of the losing side being drowned. Maxentius himself was among the dead. Constantine marched in triumph into Rome. His victory that day would soon lead to an end of the official persecution that Christians had regularly suffered, including recently under Diocletian, and prepared the path that would lead to Christianity becoming the official religion of the Roman Empire, which was in turn a huge step to Christianity becoming the global religion that it is. There are many 'what ifs' in history, but the question of how history might have been changed if Constantine instead had died that day is a huge one.

Constantine's Churches

In an old pagan
city new churches are born
their children global.

Many people would draw a distinction in their minds between classical architecture and medieval architecture and would instinctively link church architecture more closely with the medieval period. Yet in reality the architecture of many churches around the world, not just those of assorted neo-classical designs, owes a huge debt to Roman architecture and to Constantine. Church buildings from before Constantine's time were, due to the frequent persecutions of Christians, usually small and discreet, like the small 3rd-century house church in Dura-Europos. With Constantine's accession to the imperial throne, that would change and change fast. The Roman basilica (from a Greek word meaning 'royal') had developed through the period of the Republic and Empire as a sort of hall for official or imperial use divided up by rows of columns, with an area, perhaps a rounded apse, where presiding officials might sit. When Constantine decided to construct churches in Rome to proclaim his vision of Christianity as the Empire's spiritual future, his architects adapted this design for three huge, architecturally magnificent Christian basilicas, the original St. Peter's, S. Paulo Fuori le Mura, and S. Giovanni in Laterano. The fundamental Christian basilica with nave and side aisles separated by columns became, with the addition of a transept to create a cross-shaped floor plan, the basis of most medieval churches.

Arius and Nicaea

The emperor wants
to know for sure divine truths
a council is called.

As Christianity started to become the dominant religion of the Empire, the question of defining exactly what Christianity stood for started to become more urgent. In early 4th-century Alexandria, a priest called Arius started publicising his views on Jesus and God. He did not see them as equal and one, as in the concept of the Trinity. He saw God as one, but saw Christ as created by God. His views attracted considerable interest and support. They also created considerable opposition from those who thought they undermined a central tenet of Christianity. Constantine decided the question urgently needed sorting out and he called a meeting of bishops, which met in 325 at Nicaea, in what is now Turkey. The Council of Nicaea would examine a number of problems with which the Church was wrestling. Most pressing though was the question of Arius. In the end, the council condemned Arius and his ideas, and created an agreed statement of faith which described the fundamentals of Christianity as they saw them, a creed. Arius himself would die in 336 but neither this nor the condemnation at Nicaea ended Arianism. The emperors Constantius II and Valens, for instance, were sympathetic to Arianism, and a number of Germanic tribes, when they converted to Christianity converted to Arian Christianity. Gradually though, through the late 4th century and early 5th, Arianism was ousted from mainstream Christianity.

Constantinople

Town of west and east.
Gold gleaming it will live long
after both empires.

For many centuries, the Greek city of Byzantion or Byzantium stood on the site of what we now call Istanbul. In 196, it had the misfortune to pick the wrong side in a civil war, and ended up being burnt by Septimius Severus and renamed Augusta Antonina. The name Byzantium, however, lived on and still, of course, lives on today when we talk of the Byzantine Empire. In 330, however, Constantine both changed the name of the city and transformed its future. Roman emperors had long struggled with the problem of controlling the vast space occupied by the Empire. Constantine decided he needed a new Christian centre of government that could give him convenient access to both central Europe and the east. After a vast construction programme the new city was consecrated in 330. Constantine called the city New Rome, but it become known as Constantinopolis, the City of Constantine, or Constantinople. Apart from its position, of course, not that much had changed from the old Rome. The new Rome would still have its circus, its baths, its brothels, its violence and its imperial skulduggery.

Cataphracts

Rome's armoured knights sheathed
in dragon scales, sun shining,
a deathly deep bite.

One of Rome's strengths as it had expanded the territory it controlled during the Republic and Early Empire was a very pragmatic approach to sourcing the kit and tactics it needed to win on the battlefield. Where they could find non-Roman examples of either that would prove useful in a fight, the Romans often adopted them. And this process continued in the later Empire. Many people tend to think of the knight, heavily armoured, galloping across the battlefield lance raised, as an invention of the Middle Ages, but the Romans had their own version, the cataphracts (from the Greek for armoured) and yes, they borrowed the idea from elsewhere. In their wars against the Dacians and Sarmatians and the Parthians and Persians, the Romans encountered men and horses almost totally covered in scale armour. Having been on the receiving end, the Romans formed their own units of these cataphracts, which in battle could act almost as the tanks of the ancient world. By the early 2nd century the Romans had their own *ala I Gallorum et Pannoniorum catafractata* and in the 3rd and 4th centuries there are a significant number of references to cataphracti and cataphractarii in the Roman army.

Julian, Paganism and the East, 361-363

Classical dreaming
your pagan counter-attack,
lost in Persian sands.

It would be easy to think because of modern interest in Constantine's promotion of Christianity that somehow during his reign he made the whole Empire suddenly Christian. He didn't. Flavius Claudius Julianus, the son of Constantine's half-brother, was brought up a Christian but studied at Pergamum, Ephesus and Athens, fell in love with classical Greek culture and converted to paganism. He thus acquired the name by which he has mostly been known to history, Julian the Apostate. The dynasty founded by Constantine had become a messy affair and in 354 Julian's cousin, the emperor Constantius II after the execution of his previous Caesar or deputy emperor, appointed Julian to the job. Julian distinguished himself militarily in Gaul fighting invaders and on the death of Constantius became emperor in his place. Imperial favour now switched from Christianity to paganism. Julian attempted to weaken Christianity and to strengthen paganism to counter it. He had limited success in both attempts. He had, however, even less success in the main military effort of his reign. In 363 he led a massive Roman army, with accompanying fleet, to attack the Persians. They crossed the Euphrates and took assorted towns until they reached Ctesiphon near Baghdad. Unable to take the city quickly and harried by Persian guerrilla attacks, Julian eventually reluctantly agreed to retreat. During the retreat Julian, the last emperor of Constantine's dynasty, was hit by a spear and died. His successor, Jovian, was a Christian.

Slaughter at Adrianople, 378

An emperor's blood
stains horses' hooves richest red
old foe new future.

In 251 the Goths had destroyed a Roman army and killed a Roman emperor. In 378 they would do it again. In the 370s the Huns were already on the move to the north of the Goths, smashing into the Goths' territory and forcing them south. The Goths sent an envoy across the Danube asking the emperor Valens to give them asylum within the Empire. The Romans knew well that the Goths could fight and Valens saw the Goths as a source of ready-made auxiliary troops he could use to boost his own forces, stretched by multiple threats. He had had previous friendly contact with a Visigothic leader called Fritigern. Consequently, he gave permission for Fritigern and his followers to cross. The local Roman authorities, however, lost control of the situation and Goths and others, perhaps in their hundreds of thousands, crossed into the Empire. When local Roman officials then tried to cheat and abuse their newly arrived guests, violence erupted. A huge Gothic army started ravaging the neighbourhood. The emperor Valens marched westwards from Antioch to fight this new threat. His forces met the opposing forces including Visigoths, Ostrogoths and others at Adrianople, west of Constantinople, on 9 August 378. The strength of the Gothic cavalry proved decisive, smashing aside the Roman cavalry. By the end of the battle, perhaps two-thirds of the army of the east had been killed, along with the emperor himself, and the Goths were inside the Empire. An eventual peace deal would allow them to remain there, theoretically subject to Roman control and with obligations to supply fighters for Rome, but in practice, almost independent. The cutting up of the Western Empire had begun in earnest.

Mag Max, Rebel Emperor, 383-388

Great by name bigger
your ambitions Maximus
five year maximum

OK, the rebel emperor Magnus Maximus didn't have customised road warrior vehicles like that of the dystopian Mad Max movie series, but many of his coins do bear the legend MAG MAXIMUS and his is a fascinating story of a rebel warrior in a society close to collapse. In 383, Magnus Maximus (a modest name that in Latin means Great, The Greatest), Roman commander in Britain, tried to do what Constantine had done and use Britain as a base to seize the imperial throne. He crossed into Gaul with an army and had at first had huge success. He defeated the emperor Gratian and Gratian ended up dead. Maximus then successfully established control of much of the Western Roman Empire. In 387, however, he invaded Italy. The emperor Theodosius in the east had had enough. His forces defeated those of Maximus at battles in what is now Croatia, and Maximus himself was killed in 388 at Aquileia in northern Italy. Many of the troops he had taken from Britain never returned home, a development that probably played a part in the final collapse of Roman Britain just over 20 years later. At least a few of his troops, however, probably did return home and Maximus would later became a significant figure in medieval Welsh legend and literature, as Macsen Wledig, Prince Macsen. A number of Welsh medieval dynasties would claim descent from him.

The Execution of Priscillian

Faith fatality
you will be the first drop of
crimson thunderstorm.

Priscillian is not exactly a name on many people's lips these days, but he would be the forerunner of many over the coming centuries. He was basically the first person to be executed for heresy. Somewhere around the year 375 Priscillian had begun to teach his version of Christianity in Spain. Priscillian preached a severely ascetic form of religion which took a somewhat dualistic approach seeing a division between some pure spiritual elements and some sinful physical elements. It was not to the liking of a number of bishops including those of Merida and Ossonuba. They eventually they took action. Priscillian's ideas were discussed at the Council in Saragossa in 380. He was still elected as bishop of Avila but eventually he would be exiled from Spain to Italy. The struggle, however, was not finished and next it was Ithacius of Ossonuba who found himself forced out of Spain. Ithacius, however, then sought the help of rebel emperor Magnus Maximus. In the end, Priscillian was summoned to Trier where he was charged with sorcery and immoral conduct, and was executed.

Symmachus and the End of Roman Paganism

Vesta's sacred flame
now a smear of smoke not by
foreign hand but Rome's.

In less than a century Christianity went from being a minority religion persecuted by the Roman pagan authorities to being the religion of the Roman authorities, who in turn encouraged or allowed the suppression of paganism. It is an extraordinary religious reversal. In 303 Diocletian and Maximian had launched their campaign against Christians, ordering them to obey traditional pagan religious practices and sacrifice. In 382, the emperor Gratian ordered the Altar of Victory removed from the senate house in Rome. The senator Quintus Aurelius Symmachus led a delegation to the emperor to request it be restored. The request we denied. The emperor Theodosius was to go much further, severely restricting paganism, and encouraging a climate in which pagan temples were closed and destroyed. In 394, the sacred fire in the Temple of Vesta that had been the sacred eternal flame of pagan Rome was extinguished and the Vestal Virgins who had tended it were disbanded. This did not, of course, extinguish the classical tradition from Rome and Byzantine. That continued, sometimes in rather unusual fashions. In the early 6th century, in Constantinople, for instance, the future empress Theodora allegedly first found fame by performing a distinctly racy recreation of Leda and the Swan on stage, involving a striptease, a sprinkling of grain in a certain area, and some geese.

Stilicho, Alaric and the Sack of Rome, 410

No longer locked out
the enemy now within
eight centuries gone.

As the 4th century wore on, there were more and more peoples originating from beyond the Empire's borders now inside it, and they and their children would have more and more effect on it. This includes both those groups prepared to work for the Empire and those prepared to work against it, sometimes the same people at different times. The half-Roman, half-Vandal general Stilicho, married to the niece of the emperor Theodosius, was appointed as protector of the boy emperor Honorius on the death of Theodosius. He faced many problems when he took over, including a rebel emperor, Eugenius, but one of his biggest problems would be a Goth who had served as an officer under the Romans named Alaric. Tiring of working with the Romans, Alaric led the Visigoths on raids deep into the Balkans and Greece. Eventually, Alaric turned his forces westwards and invaded Italy. Stilicho defeated him at the battle of Pollentia in 402. Alaric first withdrew from Italy but then returned in 403. Again the Visigoths were forced out. In 408, though, imperial politics caught up with Stilicho. Honorius has not been regarded by historians as one of Rome's wiser and more capable emperors. By now a man, and suspicious of Stilicho's power, Honorius thanked him for all his hard work by having him executed. Alaric, looking for land and money, proceeded to besiege Rome three times. In the end, in 410 he took Rome and plundered it for three days. Rome had not been taken by foreign enemy forces in almost eight centuries. Alaric died soon afterwards and the Visigoths headed west to southern Gaul and Spain where they would eventually settle.

Rebels and Invaders

A crowned head crush hour
too many emperors for
Gaul alone to hold.

While there was chaos in Italy in the early years of the 5th century, it wasn't exactly peaceful elsewhere. In Britain, the troops were rebelling. Yet again. In 407, rebel emperor Constantine III crossed the Channel into Europe with an army to seize power. At first he had plenty of success and set up his headquarters in the beautiful city of Arelate, Arles, in what is now southern France. But already it was getting complicated. Shortly before Constantine crossed into Gaul, a large group of Vandals, Alans and Suevi had crossed the Rhine and set off across Gaul to Spain. There they would set up their own kingdoms within the Empire. Constantine sent his British-born general Gerontius into Spain only to find him rebelling, proclaiming his own emperor, Maximus, and attacking Constantine in Gaul. Meanwhile Constantius, a general loyal to Honorius, was advancing across Gaul and eventually Constantine surrendered in 411 and was killed. With Constantine off the scene, a Gallic aristocrat Jovinus made a grab for power in Moguntiacum, Mainz, later signing up his brother Sebastianus as fellow emperor. They had the support of some Alans and Burgundians under their king Gundahar or Gunther (later to appear in the *Nibelungenlied*, the epic poem *c.* 1200). Honorius managed to secure the support of the Visigoths against the two new rebel emperors, even though they had with them one Priscus Attalus whom they had previously acclaimed emperor, then deposed and whom they would later acclaim as emperor again. The new rebellion was crushed, but as the early 5th century wore on, more peoples from outside the Empire had managed to secure themselves an existence, establishing their own political entities, inside the Empire.

The End of Roman Britain

Long quite UnRoman
Roman Britain Roman no
more, eagles fly home.

What is usually called Roman Britain was never actually very Roman. It had in some sense from the start been an anomaly in the Roman Empire. It was the only Roman-controlled territory separated from mainland Europe by ocean. Part of it, Caledonia, was never fully and permanently occupied by Rome and in large parts that were under Roman control, the locals took little interest in adopting Roman culture. Consequently, Rome was forced to keep large numbers of troops there throughout the occupation. Roman Britain was also, in a sense, surrounded. It had enemies to the west, in Ireland, to the north, in Caledonia and to the east, in Germany and Scandinavia. In addition, it became a thorn in Rome's side when disgruntled troops here launched, over the centuries, a series of attempts to make their commanders emperors in Rome. In 367, the Roman administration in Britain had collapsed under the weight of attacks from beyond the Empire's borders. A Roman expeditionary force restored Roman rule, but it was the beginning of the end. In the last decades of Roman rule, Rome's British armies had invaded the continent twice more, while in Britain, people formed their own militias to protect themselves. The final end for Roman control in Britain came in about 410. It is slightly unclear whether Rome withdrew or the Britons threw them out, but Roman control was finally gone. In the power vacuum left, British tribes, kings, cities turned to fighting each other, re-establishing internal borders after the years of Roman occupation, but in the process destroying much of the economy built up through the centuries in the Empire. In doing so they destroyed any chance that Britons in the previously Roman-controlled areas would unite to resist invaders from outside.

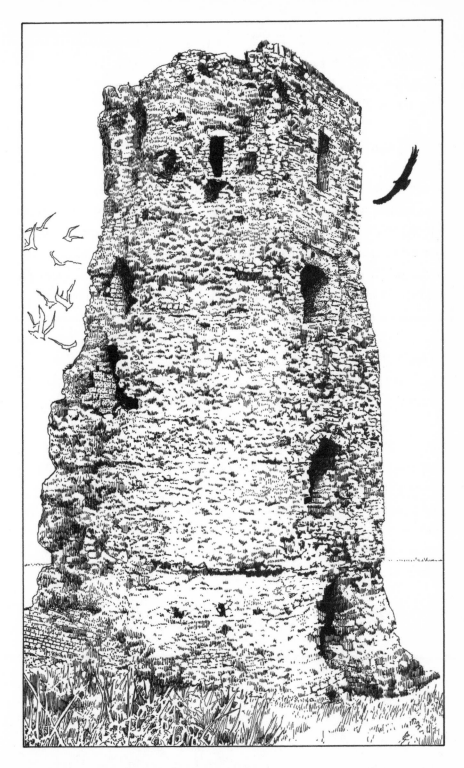

Bagaudae

Wild spirits free feed
on dying empire's carcase
fear in the country.

The Roman Empire was not built for any philanthropic reasons, but its administration had at least, in some areas and at some times, offered a sense of stability and predictability and borderless travel and communication over wide areas that had simply not been there before. However, the repeated military and political crises of the 3rd, 4th and 5th centuries inevitably had an eventual impact even on this. In some areas people realised Rome could no longer fully protect their societies. Some decided they were going to look after their own interests. The Bagaudae or Bacaudae (a Celtic word perhaps meaning fighters) were often described as simple bands of brigands by the Roman authorities. In reality they seem to have been groups of independent-minded, mainly rural civilians (most probably already experienced hunters with hunting weapons) who organised themselves in opposition to a Roman imperial administration they saw as far more keen on taxing them than serving them. They were also prepared to attack anyone else they didn't like – if you were a rich person unpopular in your local community, you were unlikely to welcome a visit from Bagaudae. The Emperor Maximian had campaigned against Bagaudae in Gaul in the 280s. In the 350s, as the Alemanni invaded Gaul, Bagaudae were again recorded as being active. In the early 5th century the Bagaudae took control of areas of Brittany. Bagaudae are also recorded in northern Spain in the 5th century.

Hypatia

Astronomy star
the sum of many talents
bright life dead too soon.

Women in the Roman Empire generally had far less opportunities than their male counterparts. Nevertheless, through sheer talent and determination, some of them still managed outstanding achievements in male-dominated areas. A particular example of this is the distinguished mathematician, astronomer and philosopher, Hypatia. She was born sometime in the mid-4th century in Alexandria. Her father Theon was a famous mathematician and astronomer and the last definitely known member of the Museum of Alexandria, a famous seat of learning over the centuries. Hypatia was to follow in her father's footsteps. She wrote commentaries on the works of famous mathematicians and astronomical tables and she was a popular lecturer and teacher. She was totally dedicated to her work and studies. She insisted on remaining single and she rejected male advances. The philosophy she taught was in the classical Neoplatonist tradition. These, however, could be dangerous times in Alexandria for anybody perceived as prioritising non-Christian ideas over Christian ones. In 391 Theophilus, bishop of Alexandria, burned down the Serapaeum, the Temple of Serapis. In 415 a mob seized Hypatia in the street and brutally murdered her, destroying the life and the career of one of the outstanding female intellectuals of the classical era.

Notitia Dignitatum

Fierce names, bright shields,
paid to die for old Rome's life
cannot save empire.

Like any well-organised empire the Roman Empire had a huge bureaucracy to keep it running. Most of the documents that were the life-blood of the imperial bureaucracy have, of course, long vanished. Not all, however. In Egypt, for instance, the dry conditions have preserved some official papyri. One of the most spectacular documents to be still with us today, not in the original but in beautifully illustrated medieval copies, is the amazing *Notitia Dignitatum*, or List of Dignitaries. The exact date of the document is disputed and it may have been updated at different times, but it was compiled as nothing less than an outline of the entire Roman administrative system sometime around the end of the 4th century and beginning of the 5th. The detailed account it gives of Roman army units and their disposition at the time is particularly interesting and useful. The document even includes carefully drawn and painted shield designs associated with individual units. It is a fascinating gem of late Roman official paperwork.

Augustine and the Vandals

You talk of heaven
while men have come from the east
bearing arms, no gifts

Arguably the most influential Christian theologian ever, Augustine was born in 354 in a little town called Tagaste in Roman-controlled North Africa. Growing up he acquired a lover and had a child by her. When his mother arranged an engagement for him to a respectable female, he was forced to part from his lover and in his writings he describes the pain he felt. He took another lover while awaiting marriage. Then he changed direction. After time in Milan where he was baptised by St Ambrose he returned, now celibate, to North Africa and became Bishop of Hippo Regius. He spent his time preaching his views on Christianity, arguing against those who disagreed with him and writing works such as his *Confessions* and *The City of God*, which are still widely read today. The Roman North Africa he had grown up in and lived in was, however, about to be totally transformed. In 406 the Vandals crossed the frozen river Rhine and headed for the Pyrenees. In 429 at the invitation of a local Roman usurper and under pressure from the Visigoths in Spain, they crossed the straits of Gibraltar into Africa. By 430 they were at the gates of Hippo, with Augustine inside. A few months into the siege, Augustine died. Eventually, the Vandals would take Hippo and establish a Vandal kingdom in that corner of Africa and on islands in the Mediterranean. In 455 the Vandal king Genseric, perhaps encouraged to get involved in Italy by Roman Empress Licinia Eudoxia who hoped for help in internal Roman quarrels, would sack Rome. The enthusiastic and thorough sack would determine how we use the words 'vandals' and 'vandalism' today.

Galla Placidia

As Rome's world weakened
you stood rock in the wreckage
empress and fighter.

The career of Galla Placidia is an extraordinary example of how a single life could both be affected by, and affect, history in the last century of the Western Roman Empire. It is also a fascinating example of how Romans and Germanic newcomers teamed up to fight for control over the Western Empire in its last decades. She was a half-sister to the emperor Honorius. In 410, as the Visigoths rampaged through Italy, they captured her. When they headed for southern Gaul, she went with them. And when, in the world of shifting alliances that was the 5th century, the Visigoths joined with Honorius against the rebel emperors Jovinus and Sebastianus in Gaul, she married the Visigoth chieftain Athaulf. After Athaulf was murdered in 415, she returned home, only to find herself married off to a Roman general, Constantius. She gave him a daughter and a son. In 421 her husband became co-emperor with her half-brother. Her husband died after a few months as emperor. She then fell out with her half-brother, the emperor Honorius and had to flee to Constantiniple. Honorius died in 423 and Galla Plaicidia fought to make sure that the next emperor of the west was her young son, Valentinian III. Aspar, a Roman general of mixed Alan and Gothic descent invaded Italy with an army and put Valentinian on the throne with his mother as regent. Her reign as regent saw two Roman generals Bonifacius and Aetius each with their own Germanic allies, battle for authority within the Empire. Aetius would win. When she died in 450 Galla Pacidia left behind her some beautiful churches and a reputation as a powerful, influential, determined character.

Germanus of Auxerre

Your orders send you
beyond Channel and empire.
Into the unknown.

Britain had left the Empire, but the Empire, or at least some of the Empire's inhabitants, did not entirely ignore Britain in the decades after that. Sometime around 429, an assembly of bishops in Gaul decided that something had to be done about the spread in Britain of Pelagianism, views that stressed the power of individual will rather than divine grace in fighting sin and that were regarded as heretical by the Church. Pelagius himself was probably British so it is perhaps not surprising that his views had attracted some attention on the island. Germanus of Auxerre and Lupus of Troyes were therefore despatched to a Britain outside the Empire. On his journey Germanus is said not only to have preached successfully in Britain against the Pelagians but also to have helped the Britons 'ambush' enemy raiders by shouting Alleluia at them so loudly that they were terrified and ran off. He also visited the shrine of the British martyr St Alban at Verulamium. The shrine of St Alban is still there now, an amazing link between Roman-controlled Britain, Britain in the period after it left the Empire, medieval Britain, and now. Germanus may have visited Britain a second time a decade or so later.

Justa Grata Honoria

Dowry of terror
crimson tears brought to your forced
wedding bitter day.

Under the Roman Empire women's choices were often heavily restricted by the men around them. Sometimes, however, even then, women would get their revenge on those men and sometimes that revenge would have major consequences. Justa Grata Honoria was the daughter of the formidable Galla Placidia and the Emperor Constantius III. Her little brother was the Emperor Valentinian III. Being a key figure in the imperial family, the question of whom she might marry became a matter of state. Any possible husband with ambitions was a threat. Her love life was therefore heavily restricted. It was not a situation she was going to put up with. She therefore started sleeping with one of her members of staff. When the authorities found out, they killed her lover and her little brother forced her to marry somebody he regarded as politically safe, a senator called Flavius Bassus Herculanus. She wasn't happy and she wasn't going to pretend she was. In 450 she appealed for help to Attilla the Hun. He saw this as a major opportunity for a land grab. He decided to interpret Honoria's communication as a marriage proposal, accepted and promptly demanded half the Western Empire as his dowry. The demand was, perhaps unsurprisingly, refused and Attila invaded the Western Empire.

Aetius Stops Attila, 451

As Europe watches
strong tree you stand firm against
the storm from the steppes.

The only character ravaging the Western Empire in its last century that almost everybody even today has heard of is Attila, or Attila the Hun as he tends to be known, almost as if 'the Hun' was his surname. Perhaps it's because the Huns were such a shock to the Empire. In 441 and 443 Attila and his Huns had launched devastating raids on the east, destroying cities, approaching the walls of Constantinople and extracting vast tribute. In 447 he had penetrated deep into the Balkans and Greece as far as Thermopylae. Then in 451, demanding half the Western Empire as a dowry (see entry above) he launched his forces into Roman-controlled Germany and eastern Gaul. This time, though, he would not find it so easy. Flavius Aetius had had a very successful career, so that he became in some sense the real ruler of the west. After multiple campaigns against Germanic groups in France he finally teamed up with a number of them and met Attila's forces in battle on the Catalaunian Plains. The location of this battle is not now certain, but it was a very important battle. Fighting was fierce, particularly for a key strategic ridge and in the end, with tens of thousands of dead, both sides halted major operations as darkness fell. Finally, Attila withdrew, his aura of invincibility shattered. He returned in 452 to ravage northern Italy but in 453 died in his sleep after a marriage feast. Aetius, a man who, had he lived, might have been the person with the most chance of saving the Western Empire, himself died in 454. He was murdered by his own emperor, who himself was then assassinated in 455.

Riothamus

You crossed waves to war
now you sail on in the grey
mists of mystery.

Most people would assume that once Britain had left the Empire it played no further political and military part in what was happening inside it in its last years. However, sometime around 470, just a few years before the end of the Western Empire, Riothamus, a 'King of the Britons' is recorded answering an imperial invitation and getting involved with his army in the complex wars taking place in Gaul at that time. Jordanes states that the Roman emperor Anthemius asked Riothamus to prevent Euric and his Visigoths taking over Gaul. He then states Riothamus came across the Ocean with an army of 12,000 to the land of the Bituriges in central Gaul. He then fought and lost a battle against the Visigoths and escaped to the Burgundians. A letter from Sidonius Appollinaris, Bishop of Clermont to Riothamus supports the fact that a Riothamus did exist who was active in Gaul at this time. What is not exactly clear, however, is whether Riothamus was a king of Britons in Britain or a king among those Britons who in the 5th century were making Brittany their home. The Ocean voyage mentioned might suggest Britain itself, but a coastal journey from Brittany cannot be excluded.

Romulus Augustulus Deposed, 476

Little Romulus,
it's done, say 'bye to the crowd
and leave quietly.

By 475 there wasn't much left of the Roman Empire in the west, just Italy and a bit of southern Gaul, and that wasn't going to last much longer. In that year, the new Western emperor, Julius Nepos, recently appointed by the still powerful eastern imperial administration made the major mistake of appointing a man called Orestes, previously a minister of Attila the Hun (not perhaps the most encouraging entry to have on your CV in this instance) to command the Roman army. Orestes swiftly used his new command to force Julius Nepos to flee to Dalmatia and replaced him with his own son, Romulus. Romulus was not about to give birth to a new Roman civilisation. He was only young and instead of Augustus as his name title, he has become known to history as Romulus Augustulus 'little Augustus'. He and his father Orestes didn't last long. Their Germanic troops demanded land and when they didn't get it, they elected one of their own, Odoacer, king. Odoacer promptly killed Orestes on August 28, 476 and sent Romulus into exile in southern Italy. The last Roman emperor in Italy was gone. Julius Nepos, in a sense the last Western Roman emperor of a part of the Western Empire, hung on as ruler in Dalmatia until he died in 480.

The Kingdom of Soissons

Empire's ashes grey
but in Gaul a red flame burns
briefly then is dead.

The end of the Roman Empire was not a quick, neat event. It was never
going to be. Even after the final collapse of Roman power in Italy there
were, amidst the new kingdoms with Germanic rulers, little pockets of
the Empire still left. In Raetia and Noricum, for instance, militias still
hoped that some day they would receive their pay from somebody in
Italy, somewhere. Among the most significant of these little pockets
was the so-called Kingdom of Soissons in northern Gaul. The emperor
Majorian (457-461) had put Aegidius in command of Roman troops
in Gaul. When Germanic tribes took control of land to the south, his
'Roman' pocket was cut off from the rest of the Empire. Aegidius tried
to hang on in this new situation. At one stage he is even said to have
been chosen king of the Franks after the previous occupant Childeric
was temporarily exiled for debauchery and went off to become the lover
of Basina, Queen of Thuringia. When Aegidius died his son, Syagrius,
took over this 'Roman' pocket and when in 476 Romulus Augustulus
was deposed and in 480 Julius Nepos died, Syagrius was still there.
Syagrius had his capital at Soissons. In about 481 the Franks got a new
king, Clovis. In 486, he attacked Syagrius and in the battle of Soissons
decisively defeated his forces. Syagrius fled south to the Visigothic king
in Toulouse but was returned under threats from Clovis and executed.
Clovis went on to unite the Franks, conquer much of Gaul, convert to
Christianity and become viewed by many as the founder of the country
named after his Franks, France.

Ambrosius Aurelianus

Last of the empire's
British sons perhaps, victor,
but were you Arthur?

The Roman Empire had dominated the west for centuries and even when it was gone, even when there were no imperial administrators left in the west ruling anywhere directly for the Empire, something of its influence remained. New Germanic rulers took inspiration and imagery from the Roman emperors of the past. Some ruled at least theoretically in the name of the emperor in the east. In Britain, a British monk called Gildas wrote of a man who rallied the Britons and inflicted defeats on the invading Saxons. The man's name is Ambrosius Aurelianus and Gildas writes of him that he was perhaps the last of the Roman nation left alive. It is a controversial passage and nobody exactly knows what Gildas means. However, it seems clear that Gildas saw this man, with a Roman name as, in some sense, having inherited Roman authority and heritage in Britain. Gildas also connects him with a British effort that finally led to a victory in a battle caslled the Siege of Badon Hill. Gildas does actually give some kind of dating evidence for Badon Hill, but again the meaning is far from clear. Badon Hill is in the later *Historia Brittonum* (the earliest source to give any details on the character of Arthur), also attributed to him as a victory. This has led some to identify Ambrosius Aurelianus as the, or at least a historical prototype of, King Arthur. Whether he was or whether he was not, he was perhaps the last of Rome in Britain.

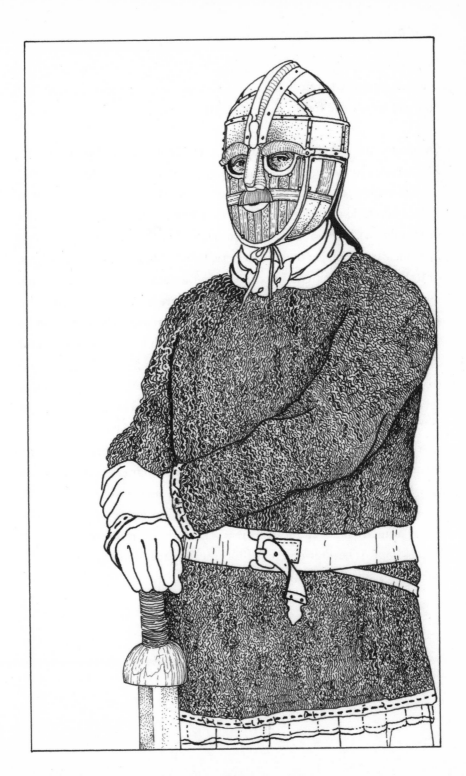

Boethius

Imperial man
orphan of empire bereft
your jail words live free.

Odoacer's rule in Italy did not last long. The Emperor in Constantinople, Zeno, had had enough of Odoacer and despatched Theoderic, King of the Ostrogoths, to despatch him. After a series of battles across northern Italy, Theoderic took Ravenna in 493. He then met for a banquet and peace talks with Odoacer, or at least that's what Odoacer was expecting. Instead, after making a toast, Theoderic killed Odoacer and became King of Italy. He would extend his control over a number of other Germanic kingdoms in the former Western Roman Empire and become known, by some at least, as Theoderic the Great. In many senses, Theoderic can be seen as a successor to the Roman emperors. Much of Roman culture and much of the imperial administration continued under him. One Roman who would serve in Theoderic's administration was Anicius Manlius Severinus Boethius, who came from a prominent Roman family. By about 520 Boethius was *Magister Officiorum* for Theoderic, a hugely important post. However, in 523 he was accused of treason and sentenced to death. It is still not entirely clear what lay behind the charge. Boethius was a very learned man, with a wide knowledge of the classics and while in prison, before his execution, he wrote the *Consolation of Philosophy*, which argued that even though the world is unjust, philosophy can still help us cope. It became one of the most widely read books in the Middle Ages and is still read today.

Justinian's Reconquest of the West

A new dawn for Rome
but morning clouds from the east
are red soaked with death.

Even when the last Roman emperor in the west was gone, there were still to be emperors in what had been the eastern part of the Roman Empire for many centuries to come. We tend to define this period as the Byzantine Empire and, by doing so, we separate it linguistically and mentally from the Roman Empire. To people at the time, this break was nothing like so clear cut. It was not insignificant that a Roman emperor no longer held sway over Rome itself, but it did not mean the end of Roman traditions, culture, heritage and aspirations in the east. At the time it was not even clear that it meant the permanent end of Roman power in the west. In the 6th century, the vigorous Byzantine emperor Justinian set out to reconquer the west. He had perhaps learnt from how the Western Empire collapsed because he sought to exploit internal divisions in the Germanic kingdoms. In 533 Justinian's general, Belisarius, landed in Africa and rapidly destroyed the Vandal kingdom there. Justinian's next target was the Ostrogoths in Italy. His forces advanced in Dalmatia, seized Sicily and in 536 Belisarius entered Rome. Italy was, in some sense, Roman again. Justinian would extend his power across much of the western Mediterranean including many islands there and much of the south coast of Spain. There was even once again a Roman presence (a little) beyond the Pillars of Hercules, on the Atlantic Coast. In the end, though, Justinian's forces would get bogged down in a long, destructive war in Italy as the Ostrogoths revived. There was to be no Western Roman Empire 2.0 and after Justinian's death, the Byzantine presence in the west would eventually be erased.

Ravenna

In Adriatic
sunlight through long centuries
gold bright beauty glows.

Perhaps few places sum up the death of the Roman Empire in Italy more beautifully (both in terms of aptness and sheer stunning visual impact) than the small town of Ravenna. It is situated just to the south of Venice, yet gets a fraction of the visitors that Rome and Venice do. An important naval port was built at Ravenna early in the Empire, called, not unreasonably, Classis (meaning in Latin, Fleet.) However, the city really came into its own in the 5th century when the emperor Honorius wanted a capital easier to defend than Milan or Rome. In 493, it saw Odoacer who had removed the last Western Roman Emperor, in turn removed and killed by the Ostrogothic Theoderic. When Belisarius restored Roman (or Byzantine) rule in Italy, in the 6th century, Ravenna became a centre of Byzantine administration. It would finally fall to the Lombards long after Justinian's death. During much of the 5th and 6th centuries amazing, beautiful churches and mausolea were being built in this place and unlike in Rome, where a high proportion of such buildings of the period would later be demolished or transformed beyond recognition, in Ravenna, which became something of a backwater, so many have been wonderfully preserved. The mosaics with their vivid colours, in particular, are stunning. It is easy to wander through the streets and churches and feel the presence of history.

The Fall of Constantinople, 1453

Last gasp of Rome's might
flies through the spring sky above
Mehmed's massed army.

The Eastern Roman Empire lasted almost a thousand years after the fall of the Western Roman Empire. Many times in those centuries it had seemed like it might become extinct, but it never quite had. For a long time Constantinople had been under threat from multiple directions. Then in the mid-14th century the Turks advanced into Europe. In 1422 the Turks under Murad II besieged Constantinople. The siege was eventually abandoned. In 1453, however, another siege would end very differently to that. The besieging forces under Mehmed II had vast superiority in numbers. They also had heavy artillery. Western aid to the besieged Byzantines was too little, too late. A chain across the entrance prevented the Turks sailing their ships into the Golden Horn, so instead they dragged them there overland avoiding the chain. On 29 May 1453 after bitter fighting, the Byzantine forces with their Genoese allies could hold on no longer and the city fell. The last Emperor of Byzantium, in a sense the last Roman emperor, Constantine XI Palaiologos, was killed in the fighting. A few ships managed to escape. The city itself was sacked for three days. The last vestiges of the Roman Empire as a political entity were gone, but its cultural legacy was already being reborn in the west, with the Renaissance.

The Legacy of Rome Today

An empire no more
Rome still resides within us
part of who we are.

The Roman Empire is long gone. More than five and a half centuries have passed since even the end of the Byzantine Empire. Yet Rome's Empire changed the world and its legacy is visible everywhere today. That legacy is perhaps most visible in much of Western Europe, where Rome brought a shared language, a shared religion and a shared sense of common identity. Rome took the learning and culture it had inherited from Greece, Egypt and Babylon, added to it and spread it across Europe and the Mediterranean basin and beyond. To the world it gave technology and architecture we still recognise in buildings today, whether they are neo-classical or churches sprung from Constantine's basilicas. On a much more controversial level its example inspired the European empire-builders of the 17th, 18th and 19th centuries as they spread trade and links around the world but also spread conquest and slaughter. Many of the effects of that process are, obviously, very much alive today. Ultimately, though, perhaps Rome's most valuable legacy is also its most personal. Its history is the history of individuals, basically not that different from us, who encountered the pain and the joy, the defeats and victories of life, just as we do today. Their stories are, in a sense, our stories.

Chronology of Some Key Events

Battle of Actium 31 BC

Battle of the Teutoburg Forest AD 9

Death of Augustus AD 14

Caligula assassinated AD 41

The reign of Nero AD 54-68

Boudicca's Rebellion AD 60-61

The Year of the Four Emperors AD 69

The Fall of Jerusalem AD 70

The destruction of Pompeii AD 79

Death of Domitian AD 96

The reign of Trajan AD 98-117

Dacia conquered by Rome 101-106

The reign of Hadrian 117-138

The Bar Kokhba Rebellion 132-135

The reign of Marcus Aurelius 161-180

Devastating attack by the Marcomanni and Qadi 169

Death of Commodus 192

Didius Julianus buys the Empire 193

Battle of Lyons 197

The Edict of Caracalla 212

The Year of the Six Emperors 238

Rome's Millennium 248

Death in battle of Emperor Trajan Decius 251

Emperor Valerian captured in battle 260

The separate Gallic Empire 260-274

The reign of Aurelian 270-275

The reign of Diocletian 284-305

Battle of the Milvian Bridge 312

The Council of Nicaea 325

The death of Julian the Apostate 363

The emperor Valens and his forces defeated at Adrianople 378

The rebellion of Magnus Maximus 383-388

Vandals, Alans and Suevi cross the Rhine 406

The rebellion of Constantine III 407

The sack of Rome 410

Defeat of Attila at the Battle of the Catalaunian Plains 451

Romulus Augustulus deposed 476

About the Author and Illustrator

A graduate of Cambridge University, Stuart Laycock has worked in advertising, marketing and TV. Stuart has authored or co-authored a number of history books in the UK, including the best-selling *All the Countries We've ever Invaded and the Few we Never Got Round To*, and *Unexpected Britain*.

John Travis's first book, *Coal in Roman Britain*, was based on his PhD thesis. He holds a Master's Degree and Doctorate in Roman Archaeology from the University of Liverpool. He is an archaeologist with over 30 years' experience, and an associate member of the Institute of Field Archaeologists (AIFA). He co-authored *Roman Helmets*, *Roman Shields* and *Roman Body Armour*.

Dr Miles Russell, who kindly provided the foreword, is a senior lecturer in archaeology in the Faculty of Science and Technology at Bournemouth University and a Fellow of the Society of Antiquaries of London. His research and publications focus on the prehistoric and Roman periods and he is currently involved in fieldwork across southern Britain. Miles is a regular contributor to television and radio.

Also available from Amberley Publishing

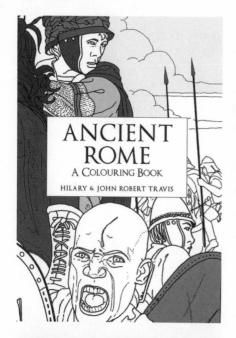

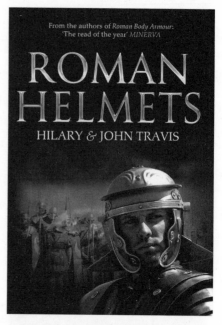

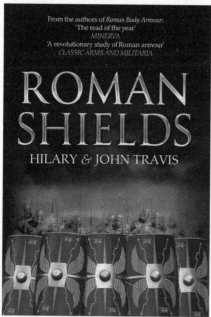

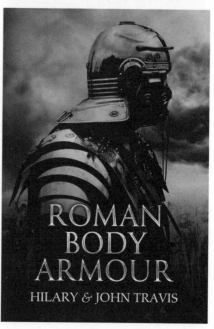

Available from all good bookshops or to order direct
Please call **01453-847-800**
www.amberley-books.com

Also available from Amberley Publishing